What I Have Learned...
(or "Nonagenarian Natterings")

Earle F. Zeigler
Ph.D., LL.D., D.Sc., FNAK

 www.trafford.com

North America & international
toll-free: 1 888 232 4444 (USA & Canada)
phone: 250 383 6864 ♦ fax: 812 355 4082

Dedication

To Anne:
"the one who has brought so much love
and joy into my life…"

Conceptual Index

Preface

What I Have Learned …(or *"Nonagenarian Natterings")* might be termed a sequel to my *Through the Eyes of a Concerned Liberal* that was published in 2004. Frankly, I didn't think I'd live long enough to have a sequel, but here it is 2012–I did! So here it is… Actually I'm running out of topics to write about– i.e., topics about which I feel knowledgeable enough to make good sense. This "sequel", therefore, explains what I believe about various aspects of "life and living", why I believe what I do; and what I sought to do about "it all." It could prove interesting to anyone facing the same or similar "life problems" in this crazy world becoming more scary as I write these words

The world situation really has me very worried. I know I'm not alone in this matter. I suppose this is especially so because the Internet, television, and a plethora of newspapers puts me in "the thick of things" pictorial-wise and word-wise roughly 16 hours a day, seven days a week. I could cut back on such extensive and intensive involvement, but there's a "contagion" about it all that keeps me ready to leap into the fray regularly almost automatically. Daily I look ahead to the immediate problem and/or hazard confronting humankind at various points on this globe that we call Earth …

Although Canada's "multicultural experiment" on planet Earth appears basically to be a good idea as we look to the future in a "migrating world," it's quite an "unbalanced mix" culturally here in Richmond where I live. However, as I "check out" the world daily through the multi-media arrangement that is available to us now, I do believe we (Anne Rogers and I) are very fortunate to be living *here* in Canada *at this time* for a number of reasons.

I'm editing this preface in Richmond, British Columbia, Canada on August 18, 2011. On Saturday, August 20, I will be 92 years old. Born in New York City in 1919, how I ended up so far from my birthplace is a pretty good yarn in itself. (However, that rudimentary tale is in my unpublished autobiographical e-book titled *Going Out a "Winner" and a "Loser".)* I look in my bathroom mirror daily and voicelessly ask myself: "How did you ever manage *to*–and find the enthusiasm *for*–completing 70 very active years in your field of physical activity and health education within the education profession?" Any way one chooses to look at it and answer this rhetorical question, I'm a very lucky guy-no matter **WHAT** happens to me from here on out… Hence I am not very worried for myself. How could I be?

9

However, what about the future of my wife, Anne; my daughter, Barbara; and my grandson, Kenan? They are, respectively, roughly 20, 30, and 70 years younger than I—and., further, what about the lives of the rapidly expanding, unbelievable number of people that will undoubtedly follow them?

The University of Western Ontario in London, Ontario, Canada finally eased me out the door forever at age 69. (Western may be characterized as a really magnificent growth story for an institution now so far removed from what it was when I first darkened it doors in July of 1949.) My last four years there from 1985 to 1989 were really part-time ones because my final year's salary (i.e., 1984-85) was divided into five parts). Hence for that five-year period I taught one undergraduate course each fall for those five years for one fifth of my 1984-1985 salary. Then, from early December each year, I was free to do whatever I wanted, professionally engaged or otherwise, until the next September...

With some exceptions (e.g., *Who Knows What's Right Anymore*, 2002; *Whatever Happened to the Good Life?*, 2002; *Through the Eyes of a Concerned Liberal*, 2004), my writing has been related to the field of physical activity education, including related health and safety information. In addition, I have also written a great deal about competitive sport at the various levels of competition. In my early professional life, starting in 1948 after I had worked in the field for seven years, I first began to write articles for scholarly journals. (There was also the odd newspaper or magazine article or column.) My first published article discussed human body types. It appeared that year, 1948, and today some 432 articles more have been published since than eventful day in my life. What they added up to, along with some 55 books and monographs, and the possible influence they all may have had on the field of physical activity education within education and the field of competitive sport—either within education or in the public sector—is questionable. Both are in "big trouble" based on what "comes through the lenses of my aging eyes." How I view the arrival, or continuation of, their "time of troubles" is explained time and again, almost ad nauseam, in my various writing efforts.

More recently, due to the serious problems that continue to emerge in society at all levels and in all sectors of America and Canada—and which thus inevitably landed at my doorstep as a dedicated professional in the field—I have taken to the writing of so-called *trade* books in addition to those of possible interest to my colleagues. These efforts—neither texts nor intensely scholarly books—are intended for general public consumption in what is probably a vain effort to correct the prevailing situation. I made a decision. The two major problems I will continue to address—from here on out—are simply this: (1) the fact that *physical activity education* for the very large majority of children is either fair, poor, or non-existent—hence this situation must be improved; and (2) *"varsity", competitive sport for the few* in education is doing quite well (thank you…), and *competitive sport in the public sector* has "run rampant", and may actually be doing more harm than good! In both instances sport must be brought back into line because what is happening is just not right, and it coincidentally affects my first major problem just addressed about the vast majority of children and youth being neglected!

Everything considered, I decided to once again vary from my "proclamation" in the paragraph immediately above. What I say here should be easily intelligible to any reasonably intelligent, concerned member of North American society facing a similar environment. First I offer my "historical interpretation laced with philosophical under girding", and then I tell how I decided that human civilization should be accepted as an adventure. The future seems so uncertain that I simply don't see how it can be regarded otherwise…

Next I explain how I entered the "realm of life assessment" as I sought to find a purpose for my life. This was "tricky" and difficult to accomplish because of the "conflicting miasma" of ethical values and problems out there confronting a person moving along in early maturity. At that point I found that I was aided by the fact that—as I entered adolescence-my mother remarried, this time to a Baptist minister. The subsequent conservative environment with which I was confronted indubitably propelled me in the direction of social and political liberalism! This occurred even though it wasn't until my liberal arts and science college education "kicked in" a bit later to solidify many beliefs that have remained with me to this day.

Next I explain the various aspects of my orientation to the philosophical stance known as pragmatism. Acceptance of this position while a young university instructor simultaneously working toward a doctor of philosophy degree in education served to "solidify" my acceptance of political and social liberalism as guidance throughout the course of my life. I followed with an explanation of my ongoing desire to be liberally educated myself and to promote liberal education for all.

This brought up the ever-present need to make "defensible ethical decisions" based on a wise choice of values. This matter was confounded by what I gradually saw as the ever-increasing need to counteract America's value orientation as the world moves along in the 21st century. To do this I had to reassure myself that I was on the right track. I did this by "finding myself" once again in regard to (1) my philosophic self-evaluation, (2) my socio-political self-evaluation, and (3) my personal, recreational self-evaluation. (The reader may wish to "experience" these self-evaluations for himself/herself; so I made theme available as appendices.

Then, as this "minor opus" of "Natterings" was drawing to a close, my penultimate chapter is devoted to an "exhortation" where I encourage North Americans to re-examine their values as they embrace what I term a modified form of postmodernism. To me this belief is so vital as we all transverse pathways leading to uncertain future.

Finally, I close with some thoughts that are more personal. All of these incursions *into* what occasionally is "foreign territory" for me in my continuing effort to "*size things up*" are simply an effort by one fallible creature to "*figure things out*"! Such an overall survey of my "internal landscape" in this book represents a sincere effort to offer some definitive analyses of me and my various pursuits.

I have been kvetching about all this for a very long period of time. I have worked hard; I have been an interested observer; and I have been a concerned citizen, as well as a diligent member of the education profession serving in four different universities (in one twice) in America and Canada. Finally, I can only hope that America will "come to its senses", but "sitting here relatively safe and sound in Canada," I must say sadly that I won't be "holding my breath…"

Earle F. Zeigler,
Richmond, BC, Canada,
2012

Selection 1
Interpreting History Philosophically

My endeavors in the writing of history have been accompanied typically by philosophical "under girding." When I first became really interested in history more than 70 years ago, I examined carefully the various approaches to historical interpretation employed in the twentieth century. A bit later, when I became interested in philosophy as well, I did something similar with this discipline. In retrospect, there have been interpretations where historians, for example, treat the rise and fall of separate civilizations with an accompanying analysis of the rationale underlying such evanescent development (e.g., Toynbee, Spengler).

In similar fashion, but somewhat differently, Hegel and Marx sought to develop sets of rules or principles by explaining the continuous change that occurs in all civilizations. Other historians (e.g., F. J. Turner) uncovered hitherto unknown factors that moved a society's development in one direction or another. Still others argued that historical research should (and could) be more objective and scientific (e.g., Ranke). A fifth approach, taken by historians who believed almost the opposite, reasoned that history could never obtain true objectivity and should therefore be as contemporaneous as possible.

Finally, there have been those who were pragmatic and pluralistic in their historical endeavors. These scholars typically believed that a multiplicity of causative factors underlay historical development. Accordingly, they assumed an intermediate position. Hence, they avoided dogmatic theories and agreed generally that perfect objectivity was not possible. With this last approach, there has been a tendency to employ ad hoc any general theory that appeared to explain a historical point or occurrence reasonably well (Handlin, 1967, pp. 15-21).

One of the most interesting, insightful, and readable discussions about "ideas in history" that I discovered early on came from Allan Nevins many years ago. In his *The Gateway to History* (1963), he stated that society was controlled in the past by both practical and philosophical ideas. Practical ideas, as he explains it, express "immediate mundane aims" and are brought to fruition by certain human beings exerting their will upon others. Examples of this would be (1) the concept of 'nationalism', (2) the divine right of kings, (3) the idea that a religious leader should have greater control than a temporal power over people's lives—*or even (4) the unique idea that the people should decide their own destiny at the ballot box...*

Philosophical ideas, in contrast to those in history, are theoretical and may typically not be judged by any pragmatic test. However, many people in a given society may tend to accept that one specific doctrine is true. The ancient Greeks, for example, believed that Fate (Moira) ruled the destinies of both gods and men. With ideas of this type, however, there was no effort to validate the thought by practical results. Another example of this, Nevins explained, would be the devastating result that would occur if people (in the Western world at least) gave up on the idea that there might be an afterlife. A further example of an important, relatively modern philosophical idea is that of progress as a concept or belief (pp. 261-262).

The Complexity of Philosophy of History

We can now begin to understand more clearly how complex philosophy of history is or can be. This is why there is good, bad, and indifferent history. This is also why students should read excellent, well-written history when they are at all levels of their education and then continue in this fashion throughout their lives. The best history is more than the recounting of innumerable facts and events in sequential order. It is *the interpretation and synthesis of the facts* that are gathered that can make history vital, dull, or almost useless. However, even if step one (fact-gathering) is well done, and step two (interpreting and synthesizing the data) is carried out by a discerning mind, it is still essential that the historian have the ability to write interestingly, well, and vividly.

It is both interesting and significant that only two of the principal philosophies of Western history were expounded before 1700 (i.e., the Greek/Roman philosophy of history that Fate ultimately ruled all, and the Christian philosophy of history in which St. Augustine declared that there was a divine purpose for God's creatures. Thus, in modern times there has been a succession of philosophic interpretations of history beginning with Voltaire's belief that the past can be interpreted rationally. This was followed by Hegel's promulgation that an epoch is typically dominated by an idea (thesis) which is rebutted (antithesis), and after a "theoretical struggle" a new idea (synthesis) is formed.

Then, in the 1850s, Darwin announced his theory of natural selection, and the field of history has not been the same since. This is not to say that the concept of progress in the sense of some sort of evolution had not been thought of earlier, but there can be no denying that Darwin gave the idea more definite direction. This idea has been challenged, of course, by Marxist historians who may be said actually to be espousing a philosophic stance-that the theory and practice of economic production actually determines the other characteristics of the entire political and social system. Others have subsequently carried this doctrine to the extreme, far beyond the designation of the means of production as the dominant factor in a society social condition. Nor did Marx and Engels deny the influence of ethical or spiritual factors on society, or the possible influence of great leaders; they simply argued that morality emanates from the "social engagement" of men and women, and that economic factors impact greatly upon all aspects of a culture (Nevins, pp. 261-275).

The 20th century witnessed the emergence of a variety of treatises in which the development of civilization has been characterized as being shaped by almost rhythmic phases. Without denying that evolutionary forces were involved, theoretic formulations have been postulated in which, to a greater or lesser extent, supernatural power may be directly or indirectly involved (e.g., Spengler, Toynbee, Sorokin, Pareto). What did the late Will and Ariel Durant (1961) think about all this? They said: "History smiles at all attempts to force its flow into theoretical patterns or logical grooves; it plays havoc with our generalizations, breaks all our rules; history is baroque." (p. 267)

Toynbee's Traditional Philosophy of History

Nevins (1963, p. 271) believed that "Toynbee's has been by far the most arresting and influential [force]." Without committing ourselves (i.e., as the writer or the reader) to any particular philosophy of history, let us follow this recommendation about the work of the late, eminent British historian. Thus, the remainder of this brief examination of the topic will offer a summary of Toynbee's historical analysis. Toynbee (1947) postulated that the story of humankind may be told through the life of 21 major "civilizations" (p. 34). We learn that five of these civilizations are still alive, but that only Western civilization is still relatively healthy (p. 8). The other four—Far Eastern, Hindu, Islamic, and Orthodox Christian (largely

U.S.S.R.)–are weakening and are being incorporated into a "Great Society" with a Western shading (Zeigler, 2009, pp. 55-61).

Civilization's Pattern of Growth

Most civilizations seem to have gone through a fairly identical pattern of birth, growth, breakdown, and disintegration. A society is but a group of individual humans with an infinite number of interrelationships. It could go on indefinitely, although none has to the present day. Toynbee parted company with Spengler, who believed that a civilization is an organism whose life path is predetermined. Toynbee denied also the theory that a superior race is necessary to found a civilization (p. 55), or that a civilization is created only by a most favorable environment (p. 57).

Themes of Action

Toynbee endows history with the possession of certain "themes of action." They all seem to have a one-two rhythm such as "challenge-and-response" as the society develops, then "withdrawal-and-return" or "rout-and-rally" as it begins to disintegrate (p. 67). Humans answer the right challenge presented by the environment and thereby are started forward on the path to civilization. This does not mean that people have the help of a favorable or easy environment. Conversely, they are confronted with many difficulties that stimulate them (p. 87). Humans develop as they respond to the various stimuli. Subsequently, the developing society faces a number of other stern challenges such as war, unfavorable environmental conditions, and other conceivable moral or physical pressure.

Breakdown of Civilization

If a civilization meets its challenges, it survives. Its life is measured by the number of challenges that confront it and are then met successfully. Trouble comes when an incorrect response is made to a specific challenge or stimulus. Then the society is faced with what Toynbee calls a "Time of Troubles." This period in the civilization's development is not necessarily a catastrophic fall to oblivion; it may–if truly serious–go on for hundreds of years. It does, however, usually result in a "Universal State" (p. 12). This occurs when the conflicting countries have order imposed on them by some stronger force. An example of this would be Rome's Augustan dictatorship.

Such a Universal State may extend over what seems to be a very long period of time, such as the 2,400 years of Egypt's two empires.

Characteristics of the Universal State

Actually, the beginning of the Universal State appears to some as the foundation of a stable society. In reality it is a symptom of the disintegration of the society, since the people no longer follow the rulers of their own accord. This period of decline is accompanied by a "wanderings of peoples," as occurred in Europe when the Roman Empire waned. One of the characteristics of such a period may be the adoption of a new religion by the proletariat. For example, consider the growth of the Christian Church, which developed into a Universal Church (p. 24). Subsequently, it served as a basis of a second or "affiliated" civilization. Thus we are told that Western civilization grew out of the Greek/Roman society via the Universal Church of Christianity.

In like manner, it may be reasoned that the Far Eastern civilization of China-Japan-Korea developed from earlier Sinic civilization via Buddhism. Toynbee stated, in essence, that these are the broad outlines of the 21 civilizations that the world has seen. (This theory describing the development of civilizations is obviously not agreed to by all historians. Some feel that it does not fit all civilizations exactly, while others assert that it is defective because it is derived too exclusively from an analysis of the Greco/Roman civilization.)

Progress of Civilizations

Although we are concerned primarily with an analysis of what is termed "civilization", it should not be forgotten that the mutation of sub man into man took place in a social environment more than 300,000 years ago. We should consider the idea that this transformation may well be a more significant amount of growth and development than has taken place yet under the banner of civilization. The concept of 'progress', as we think of it, is considered by most to be relatively new historically, although some historians argue that the ancient Greeks thought of it in just about the same way as we do today. Similarly, the concept of 'civilization', indeed the word itself may have first been used by the Marquis of Mirabeau in 1757 in his work *L'Ami des Hommes ou Traite sur la Population*. Nef (1979) states that the term was uses to describe "a condition of humane laws, customs, and manners, of relatively tender human relations, and of restraints on warfare which the Europeans supposed had raised them and their kinsmen overseas . to a higher level of temporal purpose and of conduct than had been reached before on this planet." (p. 2)

Toynbee (1947) used the term less specifically almost 200 years later with his interesting metaphor of civilizations having arrived at various ledges on the way up a rocky mountainside (p. 49). Each civilization is depicted by a man of that particular society at some level on the way to the peak. Most of these "men" are lying dead on a ledge situated at a fairly low level. These include the Egyptiac, Sumeric, Hittite, Babylonic, Indic, Minoan, Hellenic, Syriac, Sinic, Andean, Mayan, Yucatec, and Mexic civilizations. Five other civilizations appear to have been halted on nearby ledges. Of these five, the Spartan and Ottoman civilizations are dead. The remaining three-Polynesian, Nomadic, and Inuit-are represented by individuals in a sitting position; they are the arrested civilizations (p. 16).

The Status of Western Civilization

As mentioned above, five civilizations are still climbing up the mountain, but only the Western civilization is relatively healthy. The other four-Far Eastern, Hindu, Islamic, and Orthodox Christian-appear to be "weakening" because of Western influences. To continue with the suggested metaphor, we may ask the question, "How much farther will the Western human climb?" Could it be that our "Time of Troubles" started during the religious wars of the 16th century? (p. 245). Proceeding from this premise, it might be argued that both Napoleon and Hitler failed to create a Universal State. It could be that another great power will be the conqueror that will begin the time of the Universal State (p. 239). Of course, futurologists or science fiction writers must now give full consideration to whether any country would be in a position to exert such influence if nuclear warfare were to begin.

In 1987, ABC Television presented a controversial show titled *Amerika* that depicted the onset of decay in the United States to such an extent that the Soviet Union merely stepped in and took over with the assistance of an international armed force representing the United Nations. This appeared to be different from Toynbee's "schism of the body social" postulated as symptoms of such decline in which there were three parts known as the dominant minority, the internal proletariat, and the external proletariat. What he was describing basically was a situation in which there was "a failure of creative power in the minority, an answering withdrawal of mimesis (limitation) on the part of the majority, and a consequent loss of social unity in the society as a whole" (p. 26). This meant that often in the past a "creative minority" had degenerated into a "dominant minority," which then used force to rule because this group no longer merited respect. Certainly in our democratic society we do not find the internal proletariat becoming ascetic and ready to secede or "wander off" because a creative minority has degenerated into a dominant minority. Thus it might be that our civilization is not very far advanced on its way to disintegration–based on Toynbee's theory, that is...

Postmodernism and History

It would be nice to leave you here on this "semi-high note" about the future of humankind. However, before moving ahead, I should discuss the concept of 'postmodernism' briefly. This is an almost illusionary movement that began to gather strength after World War II during the second half of the 20th century. I appreciate that it is difficult to get involved in "the postmodernism discussion" without some definitions and landmarks. In addition, I have found a rather unbelievable amount of jargon being spouted by people from various disciplines with seemingly little consensus emerging that makes for intelligent discussion.

What is postmodernism? While most philosophers have been "elsewhere engaged" for the past 50 years or more, what has been called postmodernism, a term which is still poorly defined that gradually became a substantive factor in broader intellectual circles. I freely admit to grumbling about the term "postmodern" for decades. I say this, because I feel it has been used badly. This is the case, also, with other, once meaningful philosophic terms such as existentialism, pragmatism, idealism, realism, etc. They emerged eventually as common parlance as well as philosophical terms still used occasionally in scholarly circles.

Interestingly, Walter Truett Anderson (1996) identifies postmodernism as one of four prevailing worldviews. These four worldviews are (1) the postmodern-ironist, which sees truth as socially constructed; (2) the scientific-rational in which truth is found through methodical, disciplined inquiry; (3) the social-traditional in which truth is found in the heritage of American and

Western civilization; and (4) the neo-romantic in which truth is found either through attaining harmony with nature and/or spiritual exploration of the inner self.

Because postmodernists tend to view truth in this manner, the result is that a minority us it to challenge prevailing historical knowledge. It can be argued, also, that it is employed considerably less by the few truly seeking to analyze what was the intent of those who coined the term originally. I am personally not suggesting, as some have, that scientific evidence and empirical reasoning are to be taken with a grain of salt based on someone's subjective reality. Further, if any thing is worth saying, I believe it must be said as carefully and understandably as possible. Accordingly, the terms being employed in discussion, or wherever, must be defined, at least tentatively. Otherwise one can't help but think that a speaker (or writer) is either deceitful, a confused person, or has an axe to grind.

If nothing is absolute, and one value is as good as another in a world increasingly threatened with collapse and impending doom, as some say postmodernists claim, then one idea is possibly as good as another in any search to cope with the planet's myriad problems. This is a caricature of a postmodern world, of course, as one in which we can seek to avoid dealing with the harsh realities of all types that are facing humankind is hardly what any rational person might suggest. How can humankind choose to avoid (1) looming environmental disaster, (2) ongoing war because of daily terrorist threats, and (3) hordes of displaced, starving people, many of whom are now victims of conflicts within their own civilizations (e.g., Somalia as these words are being written)? Further, as we occasionally have heard, what rational being would argue that one idea is really as good as another?

What then is humankind to do in the face of the present confusion and often conflicted assertions about postmodernism from several quarters that have been bandied about? First, I think we need to consider the world situation as carefully as we possibly can. Perhaps this will provide us with a snapshot of the milieu where we can at least see the need for a changing (or changed) perspective that would cause humankind to abandon the eventual, destructive elements of modernism that threaten us all. Some argue that Nietzsche's nihilistic philosophy of being, knowledge, and morality supports the basic dichotomy espoused by the philosophy of being in the post-modernistic position. I can understand at once, therefore, why this meets with strong opposition by those whose thought has been supported by the traditional theocentrism of the world's leading religions.

It can be argued, also, that many in democracies under girded by the various rights being propounded (e.g., individual freedom, privacy) have come to believe that they require a supportive "liberal consensus" against those who challenge such freedoms whenever the opportunity arises (e.g., the War Against Terrorism). Yet, conservative, essentialist elements in society functioning in democratic political systems feel that the deeper foundation justifying this claim of a (required) liberal consensus has not been fully rationalized (i.e., keeping their more authoritative orientations in mind, of course). The theoretical foundation supporting a more humanistic, pragmatic, liberal consensus, as I understand it, is what is called postmodernism by some scholars.

Post-modernists evidently subscribe to a humanistic, anthropocentric belief as opposed to the traditional theocentric position. If so, they would subscribe, I believe also, to what Berelson and Steiner in the mid-1960s postulated as a behavioral science image of man and woman. This view characterized the human as a creature continuously adapting reality to his or her own ends.

Thus, the authority of theological positions, dogmas, ideologies, and some "scientific infallibilism" is severely challenged. A moderate post-modernist-, holding a position I feel able to subscribe to once I can bring it into focus, would at least listen to what the "authority" had written or postulated before automatically rejecting it. A strong post-modernist would undoubtedly go his or her own way almost automatically rejecting tradition. Such a person would be relying personal interpretation and subsequent diagnosis to muster authority to challenge any icons or "lesser gods" extant in society.

If the above assessment is reasonably accurate, it would seem that today a person with post-modernist might well feel more comfortable by seeking to achieve personal goals through a modified post–modernistic, pragmatic position as opposed to the traditional stifling position of "essentialistic" theological realists or idealists. Such a more pragmatic "value-is-that-which-is proven-through-experience" orientation leaves the future open-ended.

The hope would be that postmodern scholars, realizing this increasingly evident rejection of what we might call the "modern ideals," would relate their postmodernism to the emergence of a new, distinct period in the history of the developed countries of the world. The developing countries, seeing this increasingly global, decentralized world society as open, fluid, and emergent, would move to join in at every opportunity. This would become a world in which traditions are being overthrown as new structures emerge because of obvious economic and technological changes that are literally creating a new culture.

Speculation About the Future

The Universe and Earth within it continue their evolutional processes. Those who have studied the past with high degrees of intelligence and diligence have offered us a variety of philosophies about humans' history on what we call Earth. It would seem inaccurate, or at least excessive narrowness of definition, to deny any degree of scientific status to the discipline of history. We can indeed argue that with each succeeding generation the study of history, broadly defined, is becoming more of a science, as that term is generally understood.

We can't be sure about what the future holds. Yet, if the study of the past is credible, we can surmise that there will be continuing uncertainty. In defense of such a condition, we can argue that uncertainty is both dynamic and stimulating as it concomitantly provides a challenge to us all. What should concern us also is the amount of individual freedom we are permitted living within a type of political state known as a democracy. We still have to prove that true democracy is possible and desirable (!) over a period of centuries. The prevailing trend toward an increasing number of full-time politicians and an overwhelming percentage of indifferent citizens does not bode well for the future…

The various political communities in the Western world that are democratic political states must stress the concept of 'political involvement' to their citizens and promote this ideal whenever and wherever possible to so-called Third World countries as they become ready to make a choice. In addition to reviving and reconstructing the challenge to people within these countries, we should continue to work for the common good-for freedom, justice, and equality-for people all over the world who aspire to better lives for themselves and their children.

If people learn to live with each other in relative peace, the world may not see devastating nuclear warfare with its inevitable results. As McNeill (1963) stated, "The sword of Damocles may therefore hang over humanity indefinitely" (p. 804). However, it could be that the West and the East will no longer be reacting to each other by C.E. 5000. Possibly the world could be united into a single civilization through the agency of one "religion" or "thought system", although the prospects for such a future seem remote at present. Toynbee suggested this in his belief that religion may be the "intelligible field" of historical study rather than the investigation of civilizations. A seemingly better approach could well be the search for consensual values, values that are carefully and specifically delineated but free from the strictures of narrow and often dogmatic formalized religions. McNeill looks for "worldwide cosmopolitanism" and "a vastly greater stability" (p. 806).

No matter what we may believe about these conjectures, there is every likelihood that the goal is still a long distance away. We can only hope that a nuclear holocaust at some point can be avoided. After all, Earth is only about 4 billion years old. According to Sir James Jeans' calculation for the habitability of this planet, men and women, having survived at the rate of 21 civilizations in 6,000 years, still have 1,743 million civilizations ahead of them.

References and Bibliography

Adams, G.B. (1922) *Civilization during the Middle Ages*. NY: Charles Scribner's Sons.

Amara, R. (1981). The futures field. *The Futurist*, February.

Anderson, W. T. (1996). *The Fontana postmodernism reader*, London: Fontana Press.

Anderson, W.T. (1997). *The future of the self: Inventing the postmodern person*. NY: Tarcher/Putnam.

Artz, F.B. (1981). *The mind of the Middle Ages*. (3rd Ed.). Chicago: Univ. of Chicago Press.

Asimov, I. (1970). The fourth revolution. *Saturday Review*. Oct. 24, 17-20.

Ayer, A. J. (1984) *Philosophy in the twentieth century*. NY: Vintage.

Bagley, J.J. (1961). *Life in medieval England*. London: B.T. Batsford.

Barrett, W. (1959). *Irrational man: A study in existential philosophy*. Garden City, NY: Doubleday.

Bazzano, C. (1973). *The contribution of the Italian Renaissance to physical education*. Doctoral dissertation, Boston University.

Bereday, G.Z.F. (1969). Reflections on comparative methodology in education, 1964-1966. In M. A. Eckstein & H. J. Noah (Eds.), *Scientific investigations in comparative education* (pp. 3-24). New York: Macmillan.

Berelson, B. and Steiner, G. A. (1964). *Human Behavior*. NY: Harcourt, Brace, Jovanovich.

Berman, M. (2001) *The twilight of American culture*. NY: W.W. Norton.

Borgman, A. (1993) *Crossing the postmodern divide*. Chicago: The University of Chicago Press.

Bronowski, J. & Mazlish, B. (1975). *The Western intellectual tradition: From Leonardo to Hegel*. New York: Harper & Row,

Brubacher, J. S. (1966). *A history of the problems of education*. (2nd Ed.). NY: McGraw-Hill.

Brubacher, J. S. (1969). *Modern philosophies of education* (4th ed.). New York: McGraw-Hill.

Bury, J. B. (1955). *The idea of progress*. New York: Dover.

Butler, J. D. (1957) *Four philosophies*. (Rev. Ed.). NY: Harper.

Calin, W. (1966). *The epic quest*. Baltimore: Johns Hopkins Press.

Champion, S.G. & Short, D. (1951). *Readings from the world religions*. Boston: Beacon.

Columbia Encyclopedia, The New (W.H. Harvey & J.S. Levey, Eds.). (1975). NY: Columbia University Press.

Commager, H.S. (1961). A quarter century--Its advances. *Look*, 25, 10 (June 6), 80-91.

Czikszentmihalyi, M. (1993). *The evolving self: A psychology for the third millenium*. NY: Harper Perennial.

DeMott, B. (1969). How existential can you get? *The New York Times Magazine*, March 23, pp. 4, 6, 12, 14.

Durant, W. (1938). The story of philosophy. (New rev. ed.). NY: Garden City.

Durant, W. (1950). *The age of faith*. NY: Simon and Schuster.

Durant, W. & Durant, A. (1968). *The lessons of history*. New York: Dover.

Feibleman, J. (1973). *Understanding philosophy*. NY: Dell.

Flach, J. (1904). Chivalry. In *Medieval civilization* (D. Munro & G. Sellery, Eds.). NY: Century.

Geiger, G.R. (1955). An experimentalistic approach to education. In N.B. Henry (Ed.), *Modern philosophies and education* (Part I). Chicago: Univ. of Chicago Press.

Glasser, W. (1972). *The identity society*. NY: Harper & Row.

Handlin, O. (and others). (1967. *Oxford Guide to American History*. NY: Atheneum

Hayes, C. (1961). *Nationalism: A religion*. New York: Macmillan.

Heilbroner, R.L. (1960). *The future as history*. New York: Harper & Row.

Heinemann, F.H. (1958). *Existentialism and the modern predicament*. NY: Harper & Row.

Hershkovits, M.J. (1955). *Cultural anthropology*. New York: Knopf.

Hocking, W.E. (1928). *The meaning of God in human experience*. New Haven, CT: Yale University Press.

Hoernle, R. F. A. (1927). *Idealism as a philosophy*. NY: Doubleday.

Homer-Dixon, T. (2001). *The ingenuity gap*. Toronto: Vintage Canada.

Huizinga, J. (1954). *The waning of the Middle Ages*. NY: Doubleday-Anchor.

Huntington, S. P. (June 6, 1993). World politics entering a new phase, *The New York Times*, E19

Huntington, S. P. (1998). *The Clash of Civilizations (and the Remaking of World Order*. NY: Touchstone.

Huxley, J. (1957). *New wine for new bottles*. NY: Harper & Row.

James, W. (1929). *Varieties of religious experience*. NY: Longmans,

Green.

Johnson, H.M. (1969). The relevance of the theory of action to historians. *Social Science Quarterly*, 2: 46-58.

Johnson, H. M. (1994). Modern organizations in the Parsonsian theory of action. In A. Farazmond, *Modern organizations: Administrative theory in contemporary society*, pp. 57 et ff. Westport, CT: Praeger.

Kaplan, A. (1961). *The new world of philosophy*. Boston: Houghton Mifflin.

Kateb, G. (Spring, 1965) Utopia and the good life. *Daedulus*, 92, 2:455-472.

Kaufmann, Walter. (1976). *Religions in four dimensions*. NY: Reader's Digest Press.

Kennedy, J. F. (1958). (From an address by him in Detroit, Michigan while he was a U.S. Senator.)

Kennedy, P. (1987). *The rise and fall of the great powers*. NY: Random House.

Kennedy, P. (1993). *Preparing for the twenty-first century*. New York: Random House.

Kneller, G.F. (1984). *Movements of thought in modern education*. New York: John Wiley & Sons.

Krikorian, Y. H. (1944). *Naturalism and the human spirit*. NY: Columbia University Press.

Lenk, H. (1994). Values changes and the achieving society: A sociol-philosophical perspective. In *Organization for economic co-operation and development, OECD Socieities in Transition*. (pp. 81-94)

Lipset. S. M. (1973). National character. In D. Koulack & D. Perlman (Eds.), *Readings in social psychology: Focus on Canada*. Toronto: Wiley.

MacIntyre, A. (1967). Existentialism. In P. Edwards, ed., *The Encyclopedia of Philosophy*. Vol. 3, NY: Macmillan

Magill, F.N. & Staff. (1961). *Masterworks of world philosophy*. NY: Harper & Row.

Marrou, H. I. (1964). *A history of education in antiquity*. Trans. George Lamb. New York: New American Library.

McNeill W. H. (1963). *The rise of the West*. Chicago: Univ. of Chicago Press.

Melnick, R. (1984). *Visions of the future*. Croton-on-Hudson, NY: Hudson Institute.

Mergen, F.. (1970). Man and his environment. *Yale Alumni Magazine*, XXXIII, 8 (May), 36-37.

Muller, H. J. (1952). The uses of the past: Profiles of former societies. NY: Oxford University Press.

Muller, H. J. (1961). *Freedom in the ancient world*.

Muller, H. J. (1963). *Freedom in the Western world*. NY: Harper & Row.

Murray, B. G. Jr. (1972). What the ecologists can teach the economists. *The New York Times Magazine*, December 10, 38-39, 64-65, 70, 72.

Naipaul, V.S. (Oct 30, 1990). "Our Universal Civilization." The 1990 Winston Lecture, The Manhattan Institute, *New York Review of Books*, p. 20.

Naisbitt, J. (1982). *Megatrends*. New York: Warner.

Naisbitt, J. & Aburdene, P. (1990). *Megatrends* 2000. New York: Wm. Morrow.

Nef, J. U. (1979). *The search for civilization*. The Center Magazine (an occasional paper), 2-6.

Nevins, A. (1962). *The gateway to history*. Garden City, NY: Doubleday.

Oldenbourgh, Z. (1948). *The world is not enough*. NY: Balantyne Books.

Perry, R.B. (1955). *Present philosophical tendencies*. NY: George Braziller.

Rand, A. (1960). *The romantic manifesto*. New York: World Publishing Co.

Reisner, E.H. (1925). *Nationalism and education since 1789*. New York: Macmillan.

Roberts, J. M. (1993). *A short history of the world*. NY: Oxford University Press.

Rorty, R. (1997) *Achieving our country*. Cambridge, MA: Harvard University Press

Royce, J.R. (1964). Paths to knowledge. In *The encapsulated man*. Princeton, NJ: Van Nostrand.

Scarre, C. (1993). *Smithsonian timelines of the ancient world*. London: Dorling Kindersly.

Schlesinger, A.M. (1998). (Rev. & Enl.). *The disuniting of America*. NY: W.W. Norton.

Schopenhauer, A. (1946). The world as will and idea. In F.N. Magill (Ed.), *Master-works of philosophy*. NY: Doubleday.

Simpson, G.G. (1949). *The meaning of evolution*. New Haven & London: Yale University Press.

Ten events that shook the world between 1984 and 1994. (Special Report). *Utne Reader*, 62 (March/April 1994): 58-74

Tuchman, B.W. (1978). *A distant mirror: The calamitous 14th century*. NY: Knopf.

Thomas, K. (Dec. 1964). Work and leisure in pre-industrial society. *Past and present*, 29: 50-62.

Toffler, A. (1970). *Future shock*. New York: Random House.

Toffler, A. (1980). *The third wave*. New York: Bantam Books.

Toynbee, A. J. (1947). *A study of history*. NY: Oxford University Press.

Weinstein, M. (1991). Critical thinking and the post-modern challenge to educational practice. *Inquiry: Critical Thinking Across the Disciplines*, 7:1, 1,14.

White, M. (1962). *The age of analysis*. Boston: Houghton Mifflin.

Williams, J. Paul. (1952). *What Americans believe and how they worship*. New York: Harper & Row.

Woody, T. (1949). *Life and education in early societies*. New York: Macmillan.

Zeigler, E. F. (1964) *Philosophical Foundations for Physical, Health, and Recreation Education*. Englewood Cliffs, NJ: Prentice-Hall.

Zeigler, E. F. (2009). *Sport and physical activity in human history: A "persistent problems" analysis*. Bloomington, IN: Trafford.

Zeldin, T. (1994). *An intimate history of humanity*. NY: HarperCollins.

Selection 2
Deciding That Civilization Is An Adventure

My early study of human history told me that the "adventure of civilization" began to make some headway because of now-identifiable forms of early striving that embodied elements of great creativity (e.g., the invention of the wheel, the harnessing of fire). The subsequent development in technology (i.e., the making, usage and knowledge of tools, techniques, crafts, systems and/or methods of organization in order to solve a problem or serve some pressing societal need), very slowly but steadily, offered humans some surplus of material goods over and above that needed for daily living. Nevertheless, the beginnings of the first civilizations as we know them are actually only in the neighborhood of 10,000 years ago.

For example, we learn that the early harnessing of nature created the irrigation systems of Sumeria and Egypt, accomplishments that led to the establishment of the first cities. Here material surpluses were collected, managed, and sometimes squandered. Nevertheless, necessary early accounting methods were created that were subsequently expanded in a way that introduced writing to the human scene. As we now know, the development of this form of communication in time helped humans expand their self-consciousness and to evolve gradually and steadily in all aspects of culture. For better or worse, however, the end result of this social and material progress has created a mixed agenda characterized by good and evil down to the present. The prevailing religions are the product of the past 2,500 or so years. In addition, as types of political state go, democracy, is the youngest of infants, its official origins dating back only several centuries to the late 18th century. Hence, we can rightfully ask: "Is it any wonder that perfection appears to be a long way off?"

On this subject in mid-20th century, Muller concluded: "the adventure of civilization is necessarily inclusive" (1952, p. 53). By that he meant that evil will probably always be with humankind to some degree, but it is civilization that sets the standards and then works to eradicate at least the worst forms of such evil. Racial prejudice, for example, must be overcome. For better or worse, there are now almost seven billion people on earth, and that number appears to be growing faster than the national debt! These earth creatures are black-, yellow-, brown-, red-, and white-skinned, but fundamentally we now know from genetic research that there is an "overwhelming oneness" in all humankind that we dare not forget (Huxley, 1967).

The Ways Humans Have Acquired Knowledge

Royce (1964) stated that there are notably four basic means whereby people sought to surmount the obstacles preventing them from acquiring fact, knowledge, and wisdom about the universe, about Earth within it, and about people and other creatures residing on this planet:

(1) thinking, that has become known as rationalism
(2) intuiting or feeling, that is designated as intuitionism
(3) sensing, that means of knowing called empiricism
(4) believing, that tendency of humans to accept as truth that which is stated by a variety of presumably knowledgeable people--an approach known as authoritarianism

Four "Historical Revolutions" in the Development of the World's Communication Capability

As we move along with our consideration of the ongoing change that has taken place throughout history, the developments in communication are such that we humans can only marvel at the present status of opportunity for human growth that has been created. Isaac Asimov has delineated four of these stages as follows:

(1) the invention of speech,
(2) learning to write,
(3) mechanical reproduction of the printed word, and now
(4) development of relay stations in space creating a blanketing communications network that is making possible a type of international personal relationship hitherto undreamed of by men and women (Asimov, 1970).

As various world evils are overcome or at least held in check, scientific and accompanying technological development will be called upon increasingly to meet the demands of the exploding population. Gainful work and a reasonable amount of leisure will be required for further development. Unfortunately, the necessary leisure required for the many aspects of a broad, societal culture to develop fully, as well as for an individual to grow and develop similarly within it, has come slowly. The average person in the world is far from acquiring full realization of such benefits. Why "the good life" for all has been seemingly so slow in arriving is not an easy question to answer. Of course, we might argue that times do change slowly, and that the possibility of increased leisure has really come quite rapidly once humans began to achieve some control of their environment.

Of course, there have been so many wars throughout history, and there has been very little if any let-up in this regard down to the present. Sadly, nothing is so devastating to a country's economy. Also, in retrospect, in the Middle Ages of the Western world the power of the Church had to be weakened to permit the separation of church and state. This development, coupled with the rising humanism of the Renaissance in the latter stages of that era, was basic to the rise of a middle class. Finally, the beginnings of the natural sciences had to be consolidated into real gains before advancing technology could lead the West into the Industrial Revolution (Toffler's "Second Wave").

Admittedly, permitting a conscious choice between alternatives goes so far as permitting the presence of "population pockets" where there is a demand to give creationism co-equal status with the teaching of a Darwinian long-range approach to human evolution in the schools. As humans we, who tend to think we are "the greatest," may be excused from wondering occasionally why the "Creator" took such a long and laborious route with so many odd variations of flora and fauna to get to this point of "present greatness." The power that these advantages provided humans was steadily combined with technological advancement, but somehow only offered minimal levels of freedom. As mentioned above, the early development of language as a means of communication was vitally important. This distanced sub–humans even more from the apes as cultural evolution became much faster than biological evolution. In a sense, culture brought with it "good news" and "bad news." The bad news was that humans are now to a large degree trapped in a world that they themselves created. Fixed habits and

31

beliefs are strong inhibitors of change, growth, and what might be called progress.

The good news is that, very slowly, change did occur; growth did take place; and to most people such change and growth represented true progress. For example, prehistoric humans did interbreed, and in this way broadened their genetic base. In the final analysis this lends credence to the present-day argument introduced above that humans today—brown. yellow, red, black, and white--are indeed one race. This fact helps us to appreciate the development of worldwide cultural evolution. Unfortunately, however, progress has never been a straight-line affair. In the final analysis, this must be the answer for those of us who idealistically thought that the world would be in quite good shape by the year 2000! It may also provide some solace to those of us who wonder why education finds it so difficult to get sufficient funding; why professors in so many countries must often assume a "Rodney Dangerfield complex". Little wonder that physical activity education, including educational sport, despite consistently mounting evidence of the "worthwhileness" of developmental physical activity--so often finds itself in dire straits within the domain of education and then in the eyes of the public as well.

World society is obviously in a precarious state. It is therefore important to view present social conditions globally. Throughout this volume–because of my professional experience in the field–I will be emphasizing that competitive sport has developed to a point where it has worldwide impact, and also human physical activity should be so organized and administered that it truly makes a contribution to what Glasser (1972) identified as "Civilized Identify Society", This is a state in which he envisions that the concerns of humans will again focus on such concepts as 'self-identity,' 'self-expression,' and 'cooperation.'

Postulating that humankind has gone through three stages of society already (i.e., primitive survival society, primitive identity society, and civilized survival society in which certain societies created conflict by taking essential resources from neighbors, Glasser theorized that the world should strive to move as rapidly as possible into a role-dominated society so that life as it is presently known can continue "wholesomely" on Earth.

Historical Images of Humans' Basic Nature

Any effort to delineate the present status of Western man and woman must include also some consideration of the postulations that have been offered concerning the basic nature of a human. In the mid-1950s, Van Cleve Morris presented a fivefold, chronological series of overlapping philosophical definitions including analyses as (1) a rational animal, (2) a spiritual being, (3) a receptacle of knowledge, (4) a mind that can be trained by usage and that functions within a body, and (5) a problem-solving organism (1956, pp. 22-22, 30-31).

A bit later, Berelson and Steiner (1964) traced six images of man and woman throughout recorded history, but more from the standpoint of behavioral science than Morris' philosophically oriented definitions. These images were:

(1) The philosophical image (the equivalent of Morris' "rational animal"). In Classical Greece, ancient man and woman distinguished virtue through reason.

(2) The Christian image (Morris' "spiritual being") which contained the concept of "original sin" and the possibility of redemption through the transfiguring love of God for those who controlled their sinful impulses.

(3) The third image appearing in sequential order on the world scene during the Renaissance was the political image (a behavioral orientation in contrast to Morris' "receptacle of knowledge" a philosophical categorization), through which humans, through power and will, managed to take greater control of the social environment. In the process, sufficient energy was liberated to bring about numerous political changes, the end result being the creation of embryonic national ideals that co-existed with earlier religious ideals.

33

(4) The economic image of the human (contrasted this with Morris' "mind that can be trained by usage") emerged during the 18th and 19th centuries, one that provided an underlying rationale for economic development in keeping with the possession of property and material goods along with improved monetary standards.

(5) The psychoanalytic image emerged in the early 20th century. Berelson and Steiner postulated the stage that was not included in Morris' classification. It introduced another form of love–that of self. Instinctual impulses were being delineated more carefully than ever before. The result was that people were led to believe that childhood experiences and other non-conscious controls often ruled people's actions because of the frequently incomplete gratification of basic human drives related to libido and sex.

(6) Finally, because of the rapid development of the behavioral sciences, they postulated the behavioral-science image of men and women (roughly the equivalent of Morris' "problem-solving organism," but with an added social dimension). This view of the human characterized him or her as a creature continuously adapting reality to his or her own ends. In this way the individual is seeking to make reality more pleasant and congenial and-to the greatest possible extent--his own or her own reality (Berelson & Steiner, 1964, pp. 662667).

The Seven Rival Theories About Human Nature

Keeping Berelson and Morris' six images of human nature listed above in mind, in trying to answer this question about human nature more precisely, I eventually decided to include also the insightful work of Leslie Stevenson. He suggested that there are seven rival theories that postulate an answer to this basic question about the basic or intrinsic nature of man (generically speaking) (1987). Each of these prognostications is saying in essence: This is "the hand that we've been dealt," and "this is how we can best react to it what it is telling us":

Theory #1: Plato—The Rule of the Wise. Following the above sequence, Plato, for example, is arguing that that (1) this is my theory about the universe we live in (i.e., his theory of another world of "existing Forms"), (2) our nature as humans as being dualistic (i.e., mind and body), (3) the belief that these Forms are ideals about the parallel world, and (4) the prescription that the only way the world is going to "make it" is if the wisest of men rule it. (Note: I suppose in a way that's what we are doing in a democracy where we elect a person as head of state for a period of time...)

Theory #2: Christianity—God's Salvation. Moving ahead to theory #2, Stevenson stated next that Christianity also had a theory about (1) the nature of the universe, (2) what humans were like in this environment, (3) how God has explained what is wrong with man and women, and (4) what he/she needs to do about it to be saved. It does seem that there are so many differences and subdivisions by people subscribing to this theory that it is difficult to spell out the "essentials." God created the universe that is "up there" somewhere in space and in time. This universe is identified with God, a deity that is both transcendent and immanent.

The nature of man is explained as a creature made in the image of God and who is destined to have control of the rest of God's creation. However, in a seeming contradiction, he/she is also "continuous with it." True Christians believe there is life after death through a process of resurrection. A crucial point in Christianity's view of human nature is that the human is free and has the ability to love while finding true purpose (i.e., love of God).

Proceeding to the "diagnosis stage" of this theory, we find that the human has from the beginning misused his God-given right of free will by initially making the wrong choice. In this way he has sinned and the relationship with the Creator was upset. Hence, nothing he/she does will bring about "perfection" in life and living. The human alienated himself from God by assertion of the will.

What is the prescription then? Humans must look to God for ultimate salvation. The New Testament of The Bible helps humanity to find a way to eternal salvation by explaining that God sent his son, Jesus, to earth to restore the disturbed relationship that developed through suffering and atonement for the evil of man. Each person on earth must individually accept "God's redemption" provided to him/her by the life and resurrection of Jesus. In this way a way of life has been provided for the true believer.

Theory #3: Marx–Communist Revolution. It is interesting to note that Karl Marx was born a Jew in a German family that converted to Christianity. Eventually devoting himself to the philosophy of Hegel, Marx believed that humankind was destined to go through certain stages of development, each possessing a "character" of its own. This was in essence a pantheistic belief asserting that God was the whole of reality. However, when Hegel's followers split into two camps, Marx followed the thought of Feuerbach that led to the belief that religion was really identified with alienation from earthly affairs. Hence, he opted for a more radical position that it was up to humans to help move the development of humankind to a new stage of development that envisioned social progress yo be tied to material rather than spiritual progress. This resulted in the ongoing application of a materialistic interpretation of history that led to the rise of the interpretation of history as being too materialistic thereby leading to the idea that capitalism must be eliminated as the prevailing economic theory.

Marx claimed that his theory of the universe explained historical development scientifically; thus, he searched for universal laws underlying social development. An "Asiatic phase" gave way to an ancient era that eventually merged with a feudal period. Then a socialistic phase set in to be followed inevitably by a capitalistic one as worldwide commerce gradually developed. Ultimately, as we know, capitalism was to be forced to give way to communism. There were laws of history operating here, he claimed, arguing that this study of history was truly a science that could be tested by evidence. His theory appears to overemphasize the materialist conception of history asserting that material life's mode of production is what gives society its "character" socially, politically, and "spiritually."

Although capitalism has its problems, it is still in an extremely strong position in the world with some of the avowed communistic countries now adopting many of its practices. However, this struggle is far from over as the gap between rich and poor accentuates with the middle class being squeezed increasingly between them in so-called developed countries. Thus, it could be argued that a type of socialism will be needed to satisfy "the multitudes in their search for a good life."

In the theory of man that is postulated with Marxism, the future is deterministic as man progresses through various stages of history being exhorted to help the process along. Some urge that the change be brought about precipitously, whereas others seem willing to let history evolve. The essentially social nature of the human is viewed as fundamental. We learn through our relationships with others. In addition, different from all other creatures, we have learned to produce a good deal of what is needed for our subsistence. Human development could be considered a social development brought about by men and women possessing a strong sense of social activism. The study of sociology is obviously extremely important.

Marx's diagnosis of the human's plight is that he/she (Western human actually) has become alienated within world society because of the gradual adoption of capitalism as the economic system to emulate. It is difficult to understand exactly how such alienation from one's self and Nature has occurred. However, we can assume that this alienation might be from what humanity has created, and this alienation is also from the basic nature of humans. It may be possible to get some help by looking to the main points of the *Communist Manifesto*. Difficulty arises, however, when we conjecture that Marx's concern would be nicely rectified by turning everything over to the State instead of leaving so much in the hands of private enterprise. However, we can understand that Marx was "loudly" decrying the abuses displayed in the early stage of capitalism when men served *only* as an economic end.

Moving from diagnosis to prescription with Theory #3 about human nature is a simple matter. An economic system where capitalism prevails is a bad development, and it must be eliminated while something better is introduced. That "something" is to be "the Communist Revolution"! The debate really warms up at this point. Social democracy is too "gentle" and "long-winded" to bring about the necessary change; so, "bring on the Revolution"! The aftermath of this overthrow would be a social system in which humans would be "regenerated" and function in a society where ideally and eventually the State as supreme power would fade away. Considered in the light of day, we cannot but agree that the envisioned end is indeed glorious. However, considering the nature of the human, we must be suspicious of this demand to "throw out the baby with the bathwater and begin all over again." Nevertheless we know that a large segment of the world's population is living in societies that claims to have done just that…

Theory #4: Freud–Psychoanalysis. Sigmund Freud and his theory of psychoanalysis are important to us in this discussion because through his work he made such an enormous contribution to people's understanding of themselves as they live in an evolving world. Freud was a scientist who evidently didn't spend much time on metaphysical speculation about the nature of the universe, He was purported to be an atheist who viewed the world as a phenomenon in which such sub-phenomena are governed by what are called physics and chemistry. Humans evolved on this planet and are presumably subject to any laws that prevail.

The subject becomes much more complicated, however, when we shift our attention to humans. Stevenson decided to subsume Freud's ideas about humans under four categories: (1) application of the principle of determinism, (2) the postulation of unconscious mental states arising from the first category, (3) his theory of the instincts human instincts or "drives," and (4) his developmental theory of individual human character.

Determinism meant that every "mental event" was a result of something previous that occurred in the human mind. The second category delved into mental states by asserting: "the mind is not co-extensive with what is conscious or can become conscious." There are dynamic, unconscious aspects of the mind that can influence action. This does not mean, however, that a Platonic dualistic theory (mind/body) of the human is true; the principles of physiology still hold sway. He postulated, however, that the mind has three major structural systems: (the *id*, the *ego*, and the *super-ego*. The drives of the id need immediate satisfaction; the ego has to do with the human's relationship to the outside world and thereby has a direct influence on any possible anti-social drives, for example, of the id. The superego, as he postulated is that part of the ego that mediates between the outside world and the person's id. It seems confusing, but the task of the superego is to supervise the ego by projecting society's moral rules and norms to help the id "restrain itself" as the human faces society daily. Simple, n'est-ce pas?

As if this weren't enough for one man's theoretical contribution. Freud also opined about the great importance of instincts or "drives" as motivating forces within the human mind. The one that has received the most attention perhaps overemphasis, of course has to do with the human's sexual drive.

We can't leave our all-too-brief discussion of Freud's work without inclusion of Freud's developmental theory of the individual having to do with human character. He theorized about the respective influences of experience and heredity as the child and youth goes through the several stages of development on the way to maturity. It is obvious that Freud presented humanity with much to ponder over on the subject of human nature.

Moving to the "diagnosis stage" with this summary of Freud's contribution, it is immediately obvious that the well-adjusted person would exhibit a harmonious relationship among the various "parts" of the brain (as postulated by Freud) as the individual confronts "the outside world." A person can talk about it glibly using the terms supplied, we know that "making it all work" to the individual's and society's best interest is another matter. For example, there is the concept of "repression" that might be used as a defense mechanism when the person is under stress and can't seem to adjust to society's demands. However, as we mature, we must learn to cope with the conditions that confront us to "maintain control" within our familial and external environments. To what extent society "may have gone wrong" is another matter.

To undertake some "prescribing" after brief diagnosis, Freud would have us maintain a harmonious state between the several "parts" of the mind. In addition, there needs to be reasonable harmony between the person and the world. Freud did not get into the question of possible social reform, but devoted a large portion of his time and effort to the psychoanalysis of patients. Further discussion of this treatment would serve no purpose in this volume devoted to human values and disvalues related to sport and physical activity.

Theory #5: Sartre—Existentialism. Philosophers identified with what has been called existentialism are a "very mixed breed." However, there does appear to be consensus that this approach is concerned with the individual, the purpose of his/her life, and the amount of freedom granted to said person. Interestingly there are both Christian and atheistic existentialists!

Jean Paul Sartre's "brand" of existentialism denied the existence of a God, and he inquired as to what that "non-existence" meant for the individual human. Most importantly this theory of a God-free universe meant that there are no such things as "objective values" that control human life. Thus, if life has no purpose, Sartre described it as "absurd." For him this meant, therefore, that the individual is free to choose his/her life values.

How, therefore, do we describe the nature of this creature that has evolved and whom we call "man"? We are here. But there doesn't seem to be any reason for our presence. This means that, since we are sentient. if we are to have a purpose we had best get at its creation. Right now we really don't know what we ought to be! However, it does seem apparent that we have been "condemned to be free." So what are we going to do about it?

The result seems to be that the human been challenged with responsibility because of the freedom somehow granted to him or her. It's sort of a "don't just sit there; move it!" situation. Hence, what we do, or don't do, assumes great importance to ourselves—and to others who may be in our path as we wander through life.

The diagnosis of the plight that has befallen man is crucial. We can deceive ourselves and say we are not free, but that would be stupid. Sartre calls such deception "bad faith," but admits that many people end up trapped in their life situations in this way.

Unfortunately, however, the rejection of the bad-faith approach does not offer the human a clear and definitive assessment of the self. Defining the self is truly elusive, because, as Stevenson (p. 97) asserts: "human reality is not *necessarily* what it is, but must be *able* to be what it is not." This seems to boil down to a case of "striving mightily" to be truly free and in the process to avoid "bad faith."

Okay… Where does this leave us when we come to the question of prescription for the individual subscribing to the existentialistic stance in life? The situation is that there are no basic values so far as we can see. So we have to figure what life amounts to all by ourselves. As an individual, therefore, I should try to avoid "bad faith" and do my level best to be "authentic" in whatever I choose to do with my life. This is the challenge handed over to us if we accept this philosophical stance. So be it!

Theory #6: Skinner–The Conditioning of Behavior. To this point the efforts included have been those of men approaching the question of human nature philosophically to a large degree. The next one included here takes a somewhat more scientific tack into what has become the discipline of psychology. Here we will condense very briefly the efforts of B. F. Skinner, an experimental psychologist, studies that led him to make generalizations about human nature from the area known as "the behaviorist tradition."

Skinner was preceded in his endeavors by J. B. Watson and others who sought to carry out their research empirically as "the study of consciousness." However, Skinner in a 1913 paper stated that they\se scholars had reached the point where they could not agree on methodology in their research. Hence, he argued that it was time to "go outwards" and study human *behavior.* It could be observed and analyzed better than the assessment of previous introspective analyses. In addition, the importance of environment in human development, as over against heredity, was singled out by Skinner. This question is still open, however, in the 21st century.

With regard to *the theory of* the universe underlying Skinner/s approach, his endeavor was simply an affirmation of thought stating that scientific method must be used to determine what nature, including human nature is all about. The search must be for uniformities and general laws that apply under all circumstances. In this way theory grows and expands as the human seeks to control the environment and thereby thrive on into the indeterminate future. At present people make value judgments and then seek to induce others to accept their stated position on "this and that" about the world. If some practice works efficiently. And effectively (beneficently) in society, that means it should be evaluated as "good." To summarize, Skinner as a scientist was searching for uniformities among phenomena looking to understanding, relating, and ultimately controlling the world.

Insofar as Skinner's study of human nature went, he viewed the individual as a whole–not as some "metaphysically dualistic creature" that is literally "unexplainable". Keeping genetic factors in mind, he looked for environmental causation of human behavior. He believed (1) that there were scientific laws to be determined that governed human behavior, and (2) that these laws explain the relationship between these environmental factors and subsequent human behavior. In assessing these statements, we are somehow left, however, with the possibility that analysis of behavior doesn't "explain it all"–that there may also be "innate factors" that come into play as well.

Reflecting on a *diagnosis* of Skinner's theory, we are confronted with the clash between his thought and that of Sartre. Skinner believes in the determinism "of it al," and Sartre tell us that we are "condemned to be free"! Are humans "free agents" or not? What a difficult question to answer! And yet we might as well "throw in the towel" if we concur with Skinner in this regard. On the other hand, however, the "loneliness" of the person in the world postulated by Sartre is "scary" as well. Whether an intermediate position is possible appears to be the question. If there was a "social cause" for my "dubious action," why can't I be held at least partially responsible by society?

Now let us consider the *prescription* stage in regard to Skinner's deterministic position at hand. The human is faced with a world that "determines" where he/she is heading. Much of this looks very worrisome indeed. Do we "give in to it," or do we work mightily to create a situation where we find longevity and "life satisfaction" as the world evolves? Skinner would have us improve the present situation by conditioning people's behavior in a variety of ways (i.e., inducements, "positive" propaganda). This all sounds most encouraging. However, there is just "one hitch"! Someone, or some group of people, would have to "call the shot," so to speak. This is indeed a tricky situation in which to be placed. I, as author, find myself of two mind as to my decision. Finally, I must opt for "the dignity of freedom to choose myself"!

Theory #7: Lorenz–Innate Aggression. Finally in this "you pay your money; you take your choice approach" I am offering here, we come to the work of Konrad Lorenz, a man who called himself an ethologist and argued that the happenings of early childhood are basic to a person's subsequent philosophical and later scientific development. This attempt to study the character of animals scientifically by describing what happens when the environmental situation of creatures changes or is altered.

The assumption was that the instinctual behavior patterns of a particular species occurred as a result of the individual's genes evolving down through the ages. Hence it is easy to understand why Darwin's *Origin of*

Species (1859) caused such a furor when the human's evolution through so-called natural selection was propounded. I won't attempt to repeat the four empirical propositions tested by this assertion. Suffice it to say that "the world" has not been the same since this contradiction of Christian doctrine,

As the work of Lorenz proceeded, he concentrated on the aggressive behavior of humans and what this meant for "the human condition." Hence as this biological scientist considered the nature of the universe, he found that creatures of this Earth had developed hereditary movements that were instinctive and innate even though many of these human creatures' drives gave the appearance of spontaneity. The four most importanr drives of feeding, reproduction, flight, and aggression combined to provide a sort of unity to human nature.

Here Lorenz's special study of human aggression is being considered—a major instinctive drive. He examined how various species had learned to "protect their territory" in order to survive down through the ages. The "necessary" aggression had its bad points and its good points, as Lorenz saw it, but overall under "controlled circumstances" such aggression may be desirable when not overly destructive.

Moving along to Lorenz's theory of human nature, it is obvious that it correlates strongly to behavior patterns exhibited by other animals. Nature's causal laws work on us too, and we deny this similarity to out individual and collective peril. This doesn't mean, however, that some people have not developed a high degree of personal control in regard to their aggressive nature. A highly interesting theory emerges from his deliberations and studies, however. Somehow we appear to have developed an almost innate drive leading to aggression toward our own species—perhaps even more so than is the case with many other animals! This came about possibly when other tribes threatened a specific tribe, and over the millennia the "warrior instinct" emerged as basic to survival. Certain types of "communal defense" may have preordained people to aggression for survival purposes.

The diagnosis of this development postulated by Lorenz may mean that literally weak human insofar as possessing deadly appendages were concerned had no need to worry especially about "human internecine warfare" before the "age of deadly weapons" appeared to present humankind with the possibility of complete annihilation and self-destruction. Hence, we seem to have ended up with a situation where one society can cause mass destruction of another–something completely out of the question and impossible for other species. (This may be a good reason for humans to follow the advice of Dr. Hawking that earthlings shouldn't be in too big a hurry to relate to species on other planets!)

Proceeding to what might be a possible prescription for the human being who conceivably might have acquired through the passage of eons an innate aggressiveness toward his *"foreign"* neighbor in a circumscribed world where "neighbors" are within easy striking distance, what can be recommended? Might it be possible somehow to eliminate this frightening aggression? We can't build impregnable walls, nor can we drugs that will always pacify us. If one culture were to try to "breed aggression out" of its population, who's to say that other groupings would reciprocate? It seems that only more self–knowledge resulting from research might help people understand their feelings and motivations better. In this way we might promote significant good will leading to international peace.

Interestingly, and hopefully, there were groups of British and American scientists, lead by M. F. Ashley Montagu and others who argued conversely against the man-is-bad view of humankind. They argue that the question is still debatable, far from having been decided convincingly that the future looks bleak for the human species. Undoubtedly the twentieth century has been a bleak one, and the beginning of the twenty-first one hasn't seen many positive signs yet of a new, more peaceful age. However, we must proceed on the basis that "there is hope yet" for a more peaceful world in the future.

Two Basic Historical Questions

To this point we know that we are organisms, living creatures, who have reached a stage of development where we "know that something has happened, is continuing to happen, and will evidently continue to happen." However, underlying my entire analysis I have been searching for the answers to *two historical questions*: First, did humans in earlier times, equipped with their coalescing genes and evolving **memes,** enjoy to any significant degree what discerning people today might define as "quality living?"

(Note: Memes are sets of "cultural instructions" passed on from one generation to the next; see below, also.)

Second—and I added this question because of my professional involvement for 70 years in the field of physical activity and related health education—did earlier humans have an opportunity for freely chosen, beneficial physical activity in sport, exercise, play, and dance of sufficient quality and quantity to contribute to the quality of life (as viewed possible by selected sport philosophers today)?

> (Note: Of course, the phrasing of these questions--whether humans in earlier societies enjoyed quality living, including fine types of developmental physical activity--is no doubt presumptuous. It reminds one of the comedian whose stock question in response to his foil who challenged the truth of the zany experiences his friend typically reported: "Vas you dere, Sharlie?")

What makes a question about the quality of life in earlier times doubly difficult, of course, is whether present-day humans can be both judge and jury in such a debate. On what basis can we decide, for example, whether any social progress has indeed been made such that would permit resolution of such a concept as "quality living" including a modicum of "ideal sport competition" or "purposeful physical activity and related health education."?

There has been progression, of course, but how can we assume that change is indeed progress? It may be acceptable as a human criterion of progress to say that we are coming closer to approximating the good and the solid accomplishments that we think humans should have achieved true progress along with inevitable progression. Although we may all wish that peace, happiness, harmony, and well-being could prevail globally, such has not happened. Prospects for such a happy state of affairs doesn't seem very likely in the foreseeable future either. Thus, to start with, I am inclined to wish forlornly that all of the clashing religious opinions and beliefs based on hoary tradition would silently go away. Then maybe prevailing world conditions would somehow begin to improve.

But this is wishful thinking unless improved institutions are created to take their place and make the entire world a better place in which to live. (Note here that I am recognizing the perennial designation of Canada--with all of its problems!--as one of the "best countries" in the world in which to live. Certainly I'm not personally complaining--that's for certain!)

By expressing deep concern as to the question: "How might we improve the planet?" I am anxious to convey the thought that it will only be through *positive melioriem*, philosophically speaking, that we humans will be able to do something to improve the prevailing disturbing, highly perplexing, and frustrating plight of the world as it struggles in the now (so tritely named) "global village"..

Implementing what is known as philosophical meliorism means simply that men and women working together in a spirit of brotherhood and sisterhood must work positively, not negatively, to make this "global ballgame" live up to the letter and spirit of the rules that are established by the U.N. and affiliated organizations. (As a former coach, I just had to throw in that 'sportspeak' terminology.)

I believe that, in the absence of a sign from on high, we simply must— by ourselves!--dredge up the apocalypse (or unveiling) of the ethical core present in all world religions pointing to "a fuller understanding of the oneness of humankind." This we had better do very, very soon. In fact we need to do this by devising institutions that improve on these present outdated relics known as "time-proven" religions.

I say this because I am inclined to believe that the achievement for "good" of many of these theistic and/or spiritualistic approaches may soon be exceeded by their negative "bads" as their proponents parry and thrust repeatedly at their presumed arch-enemies and protagonists. (Speak to Mr. Rushdie and the many other religious and political outcasts around the world on this topic.)

So what I have to offer here is not "yet another contemporary version of the now endlessly repeated moral counsels of despair," As I see it, positive meliorism (or working collectively to improve life) on the part of people of goodwill all over the world is the only way of salvation offered to us fallible humans in the absence of reasonable evidence that there is indeed a "Messianic vision" at the core of the 13 more or less established world religions.

How did I arrive at this position as my personal response to the persistent or perennial problems faced by humankind (i.e., war, famine, death, and pestilence)? As a young person, I soon realized the inherent limitations of a religious faith to which I was almost automatically bound by reason of birth. Instead of having some conception of theism of dubious historical origin foisted upon him or her in youth, my contention is that each young person should be encouraged by his or her parents to work this philosophic/religious problem out for himself (or herself) through careful reflection while growing to maturity. I believe that an individual's development and tentative "solution" about such matters would of then have a deeper, more meaningful influence on the subsequent development of his individual as a socially oriented person and as a rational professional or tradesperson in an increasing complex and changing social environment.

Having personally been raised in a largely Judeo-Christian culture carried along by onrushing science and technology, I could not help but challenge what I perceived to be the inherent weaknesses of blind faith presented by fallible humans masking (literally) in the robes of this organized religion. In the process, what I thought I had learned from philosophers in my earlier days is also not being received with anywhere nearly the same authority as previously. Philosophers, largely because of a truncated approach to their task, rarely speak to the larger questions of life and living.

So I soon came to accept a broader definition of religion, one conceived as "the pursuit of that which an educated and presumably enlightened person regards as most worthy and important in life." What I found to be most worthy was the advancement of knowledge for the betterment of humankind along with related teaching and professional service. This to me truly represented a personal challenge, and I reasoned that what I came up with should be fully worthy of a person's complete devotion.

Moreover, our culture has now become increasingly multi-ethnic and is resultantly characterized by the faiths and religious positions of all of these migrating peoples. I do respect the personal religious stances taken by many, but one soon comprehends that no one of the approximately 13 historical faiths has a corner on the market of religious truth. This situation has indeed created a highly confusing ethical "miasma," a situation where presently the thoughts of politicians, the writings of novelists, and the jibes of comedians seemed to be taking over on the subject of human values. Fortunately, however, there is a large amount of room for agreement among people of good will regardless of which faith or creed to which they subscribe. This would also be true for those who have never been involved, or are no longer involved, with some organized form of belief.

For example, I felt that we could agree that the cosmos as we know it is evolving or developing in time. It was obvious to me, also, that the mystery of this universe has already become a highly effective source of awe and reverence for many humans. Additionally, I could see as a developing young person that our growing knowledge of this vast cosmos was becoming increasingly valuable in helping us to guide our lives in an improved manner. Further, although some would debate this point, there is evidence of a type of progress through both inorganic and biological evolution.

Naively I had supposed that the world situation would improve markedly in my lifetime in the 20th century. Well, it has, and it hasn't. Fortunately, humankind is now beginning to realize that it has certain responsibilities, and accompanying powers, for the continuation of this evolution. We are gradually coming to an understanding further that the practical application of universal brotherhood, undivided by nation, race, or creed, is vital if humankind wishes to survive. Whether we can progress as we hope to do in human affairs is a moot question.

The world is beginning to understand further that a form of democratic process in human relations provides the best opportunity for a person to develop to the maximum of his or her potentialities. Additionally, we are also steadily increasing worldwide awareness that the development of any one person shall not be at the expense of the group or society at large.

As defined above, I believe that philosophic/religious growth should be basic to all human life. It is an attitude of mind and "spirit" which should permeate all aspects of human endeavor. It is challenging to us that life as we know it in this universe appears to be characterized by creativity. Thus, it is reasonable to argue that the purpose of religion is to assist with the integration of all of a person's behavior with this presumed creativity within the universe. If religion is defined broadly, we may state that a critical and developing reason is a powerful aid in the search for a logically valid religious position.

I find that I want each individual to be free to seek philosophic/religious "truth" unhampered by official creed or outdated religious dogmas. Young people in schools and university should have an opportunity to study all of the world's great religions comparatively. In this way they will remain receptive to religious truth wherever it may be found.

I argue further that most if not all aspects of life are (potentially) accessible to scientific study. This fact can be of enormous significance in the centuries that lie ahead. As the body of scientific knowledge grows, this will help to develop attitudes (as defined in psychology) that could lead to enlightened social action. Ultimately, to me this is a much truer criterion of the religious quality of a person's life than any religious ideas which are dutifully professed rote as part of a Sunday ritual.

As I see it, also, it is axiomatic that the church and the state should remain separate. Nevertheless, I do understand that it is most important for members of any religious group--*acting as individuals*--to take responsibility for positive social action. All enlightened citizens should be involved in the political process at some level.

This leads me finally to the conclusion that the hoary religious "truths" of the past are truly devoid of meaning for people facing the world of the 21st century. Some humanities scholars may believe, for example, that the "utopian speculation of the human imagination which constitutes the core of the liberal arts" is indeed a "moral counsel of despair" unless we all have "an encounter with a reality larger than the one we ourselves invent" (R. Woodman, The Univ. of Western Ontario). If Professor Woodman has had this "encounter," I am glad for him. However, I am finding that the Pennsylvania "Dutch" motto is creeping up on me fast. I am growing "too soon oldt und too late schmart."

The Difficulty of Defining Progress

Despite what has just been stated above the "forward leaps" that have been made in the area of communication, any study of history inevitably forces a person to conjecture about human progress. I first became truly interested in the concept of progress when I encountered the work of the world-famous paleontologist, George Gaylord Simpson. After 25 years of research, he offered his assessment of the question whether evolution represented progress. His study convinced him that it was necessary to reject "the over-simple and metaphysical concept of a pervasive perfection principle." That there had been progression he would not deny, but he inquired whether this really was progress. The difficulty comes, he argued, when we assume that change is progress; we must ask ourselves if we can recommend a criterion by which progress may be judged (1949, pp. 240-262).

We are warned that it may be shortsighted for us to be our own "judge and jury" in this connection. It may well be an acceptable human criterion of progress to say that we are coming closer to approximating what we think we ought to be and to achieving what we hold to be good. It is not wise, according to Simpson, however, to automatically assume that this is "the only criterion of progress and that it has a general validity in evolution." Thus, throughout the history of life there have been examples of progress and examples of retrogression, and progress is "certainly not a basic property of life common to all its manifestations." If it is a materialistic world, as Simpson would have us believe, a particular species can progress and regress. There is "a tendency for life to expand, to fill in all the space in the livable environments," but such expansion has not necessarily been constant, although it is true that human beings are now "the most rapidly growing organism in the world."

It is true also that we have made progress in adaptability and have developed our "ability to cope with a greater variety of environments." This is also progress considered from the human vantage point. The various evolutionary phenomena among the many species, however, do not show "a vital principle common to all forms of life," and "they are certainly inconsistent with the existence of a supernal perfecting principle." Thus, Simpson concludes, human progress is actually relative and not general, and "does not warrant choice of the line of man's ancestry as the central line of evolution as a whole." Yet it is safe to say that "man is among the highest products of evolution . . . and that man is, on the whole but not in every single respect, the pinnacle so far of evolutionary progress" on this Earth.

With the realization that evolution (of human and other organisms) is going on and will probably continue for millions of years, we can realize how futile it is to attempt to predict any outcome for the ceaseless change so evident in life and its environment. We can say that we must be extremely careful about the possible extinction of our species on Earth, because it is highly improbable, though not absolutely impossible, that our development would be repeated. Some other mammal might develop in a similar way, but this will not happen so long as we have control of our environment and do not encourage such development. Our task is to attempt to modify and perhaps to control the direction of our own evolution according to our highest goals. It may be possible through the agency of education, and the development of a moral sense throughout the world, to ensure the future of our species. One way to accomplish this would be to place a much greater emphasis on the social sciences and humanities within education while working for an ethically sound world-state at the same time.

The "Tragic Sense" of Life (Muller)

One realizes immediately, also, that any assessment of the quality of life in prerecorded history must be a dubious evaluation at best. However, I was intrigued by the work of Herbert Muller who wrote so insightfully about the struggle for freedom in human history. I was impressed, also, by his belief that recorded history has displayed a "tragic sense" of life. Whereas the philosopher Hobbes (1588-1679) stated in his *De Homine* that very early humans existed in an anarchically individualistic state of nature in which life was "solitary, poor, nasty, brutish, and short," Muller (1961) argued in rebuttal that it "might have been poor and short enough, but that it was never solitary or simply brutish" (p. 6).

Accordingly, Muller's approach to history is "in the spirit of the great tragic poets, a spirit of reverence and or irony, and is based on the assumption that the tragic sense of life is not only the profoundest but the most pertinent for an understanding of both past and present" (1952, p. vii). The rationalization for his "tragic" view is simply that the drama of human history has truly been characterized by high tragedy in the Aristotelian sense. As he states, "All the mighty civilizations of the past have fallen, because of tragic flaws; as we are enthralled by any Golden Age we must always add that it did not last, it did not do" (p. vii).

This made me wonder whether the 20th century of this modern era might turn out to have been the Golden Age of America. This may be true because so many misgivings are developing about former blind optimism concerning history's malleability and compatibility in keeping with American ideals. As Heilbroner (1960) explained in his 'future as history' concept, America's still-prevalent belief in a personal "deity of history" may be short-lived in the 21st century. Arguing that technological, political, and economic forces are "bringing about a closing of our historic future," he emphasized the need to search for a greatly improved "common denominator of values" (p. 178).

However, all of this could be an oversimplification, because even the concept of 'civilization' is literally a relative newcomer on the world scene. Recall that Arnold Toynbee (1947) came to a quite simple conclusion about human development is his monumental *A study of history*--that humankind must return to the one true God from whom it has gradually but steadily fallen away. An outdated concept, you might say, but there is a faint possibility that Toynbee may turn out to be right. Of course, we on this Earth dare not put all of our eggs in that one basket. We had best try to use our heads as intelligently and wisely as possible as we get on with striving to make the world as effective and efficient--and as replete with good, as opposed to evil, as we possibly can.

Here we might well be guided by the pact that Goethe's *Faust* made with the Devil. In this literary masterpiece from the pen of the German literary figure, Johann Wolfgang von Goethe (1748-1832), we recall the essence of the agreement struck by Faust with the then-presumed actual purveyor of the world's evil. If ever the time were to come when Faust was tempted to feel completely fulfilled and not bored by the power, wealth, and honor that the horned one had bestowed upon him, then the Devil would have won, and accordingly would have the right to take him away to a much warmer climate. Eventually, as the reader may recall, by conforming to the terms of the agreement, Faust is saved by the ministrations of the author. Yet, we at present can never forget for a moment that previous human civilizations were *not* miraculously saved! *Literally, not one has made it!* Thus, "Man errs, but strive he must," admonished Goethe, and we as world citizens today dare not forget that dictum.

References and Bibliography

Asimov, I. (1970). The fourth revolution. *Saturday Review*. Oct. 24, 17-20.

Berelson, B. and Steiner, G. A. (1964). *Human Behavior*. NY: Harcourt, Brace, Jovanovich.

Glasser, W. (1972). *The identity society*. NY: Harper & Row.

Heilbroner, R. L. (1960). *The future as history*. New York: Harper & Row.

Huxley, J. (1957). *New wine for new bottles*. NY: Harper & Row.

Morris, V. C. (1956). Physical education and the philosophy of education. *Journal of Health, Physical Education and Recreation*, (March), 21-22, 30-31.

Muller, H. J. (1963). *The uses of the past*. NY: New American Library.

Muller, H. J. (1961). *Freedom in the ancient world*. NY: Harper & Row.

Muller, H. J. (1963). *Freedom in the Western world*. NY: Harper & Row.

Royce, J. R. (1964). Paths to knowledge. In *The encapsulated man*. Princeton, NJ: Van Nostrand.

Simpson, G. G. (1949). *The meaning of evolution*. New Haven & London: Yale University Press.

Toynbee, A. J. (1947). *A study of history*. NY: Oxford University Press.

Selection 3
Finding a Life Purpose

My book titled *Through the Eyes of a Concerned Liberal (Why North Americans Must Wake Up Soon)* was published in 2004 as the fourth in a series dedicated to convincing people that some deep thought and drastic action will be required to cope with life in the 21st century. There were three books immediately preceding this one in my "post-retirement series". Without going into detail, the first was called *Who Knows What's Right Anymore (A Guide to Personal Decision-Making)*. The second was titled *Whatever Happened to "the Good Life" (or Assessing Your "RQ" [Recreation Quotient])*. Number three, published early in 2004, was given the title *A Way Out of Ethical Confusion (Untangling the Values Fiasco in North America* (Trafford, 2004) It was a basic primer leading to an *applied-ethics application to personal decision-making*.

As was the case with each of the first three books in my "2000 Series," all published by Trafford, it was written because I continued to find myself terribly upset about the direction in which world affairs were heading. I had also thought that the world would be a better place by the beginning of the 21st century (i.e., when I expected to die!) Because it isn't (and I didn't!), I am now continuing my argument that (1) in a number of ways we don't really know exactly what we stand for anymore, (2) we should, therefore, periodically reconsider what we think are *values specifically* in light of the changing times, and (3) we then need to assess more carefully the extent to which we are living up to these values that are often so glibly espoused.

Now that I have come to Selection 3 that in a sense begins to "look to the future," how do I explain the ideas of "life assessment" and "finding a life purpose" that I adopted some 70 years ago? I'll try to do so by a bit of summarizing. First, I have been explaining my belief that the world is in a "hell of a mess." I added to this by stating that "the curve doesn't appear to be upward." I explained further that I was devoting my attention in this book primarily to North America--and more specifically to *the* one and only *America*.

A Values Crisis Exists

Having stated so strongly that I believe there is a "values crisis" in our world today, I then asked myself "So what?" What could I do about it? My answer to myself was "Not much, *unless. . . .*". By "unless," I meant unless I (*and you, the reader, too!*) are prepared to try to do something about the situation--that is, to try *somehow* (!) to make a difference! I decided that I simply couldn't just sit around watching the purchasing power of my pension decrease as I awaited inevitable death. I found that I was prepared to make a solid effort to turn out a series of books that, if read and "absorbed," might possibly stir some people into self-reflection and subsequent action to try to rectify what is wrong. *Of course, you now know that I believe such reflection and possible action should be based on a carefully considered set of values.*

Although I am about to become 92 years old--and obviously will not be around forever--I am especially disturbed--as mentioned above--about what is happening in the U.S.A. (the country where I was born!) I believe that the (now!) world's only superpower had been gradually but steadily disintegrating within from the standpoint of human values during the second half of the 20th century. Also, I believe at least a percentage of America's total population are recognizing that America has from one standpoint quite probably entered into a downward spiral.

In 1919 I was born as a citizen of this developing country that was consistently touted as "the last best hope on earth." Now the "last best hope," is that somehow the rest of the world through the power and influence of other political powers and the United Nations will be able to persuade the United States to return to its "proper place" in the world structure. Then maybe the world would gradually be able to develop at least adequately with the help and guidance of a reinforced, stronger United Nations.

I live permanently in Canada now, having finally become a citizen here 27 years ago. Frankly, categorizing myself as a sort of refugee, I live here because I like the climate better. That statement probably sounds a bit odd because Canada is still thought by many Americans to be "the land of snow, skis, and native Indians–and where a substantive minority speak French." However, I live now in the lower mainland of British Columbia where that "white stuff is a distinct rarity. Secondly, native Indians here have an ongoing claim to a little more of the provincial land that actually exists!. Lastly, a lot of children and young people here are studying French, but the Chinese (Mandarin) language would stand them in much better stead in the years ahead. More seriously, when I said above that I liked the climate in Canada better (despite our particular "screw-ups" on occasion), that was a "play on words". What I really meant was that presently I find Canada a country in which my present beliefs and social philosophy fit much better than they do in the U.S.A. as American values—not as they are proclaimed—but are *in reality* played out today.

I have done very well in my profession as an educator over a period of 70 years divided fairly equally between both countries. Therefore, moving back and forth between the two countries was actually not a question of my liking on two occasions to be "a bigger fish in a smaller pond." There are so many things about the U.S.A. that now turn me off that I hardly know where to start in explaining my stance. For example, I am very upset about the fact that America became the first country in the 21st century to defy the United Nations by waging war against Iraq ostensibly to oust a dictator. (I do appreciate that Saddam was a tyrant who oversaw many terrible acts by his sons and other henchmen.) I won't even bring up the subject of Afghanistan at this point, or the fact that America has troops more or less stationed in some 71 countries around the world for a variety of presumably salutary purposes…

Characterizing the United States of America

However, that's not the fundamental point. The United States has set a terrible precedent in a highly troubled world by its recent actions. (I must point out that Canada did not approve the almost unilateral action against Iraq. where it then turned out that Hussein didn't have the nuclear arsenal that was given as the primary cause for the onslaught against him.) And what was next? I alluded to it immediately above. Now I should say: "Which is next?" in the parade of countries the U.S.A. is determined to democratize one way or another while exporting Christianity, capitalism, science, technology, "peace-keeping" troops. movies, and the CNN as well? Will it be Iran?

For a second example of the prevailing "climate" that disturbs me in the United States, I'll switch to the area that I truly understand. Having worked at Yale, Michigan and Illinois, I can speak more authoritatively about sport in general and more specifically about the situation in intercollegiate athletics in the States. Sport in the Ivy League and similar institutions is fine. By and large it's doing there what I think sport participation is intended to do at the university level. Competitive athletics, however, notably in those universities where gate receipts are a major factor, has gradually but steadily gotten completely out of hand throughout the 20th century. It is characterized by semi-professionalism with all of the attendant vices that inevitably creep into such programs being sponsored in so-called educational institutions. These institutions have actually lost their "educational souls," a term that should be self-explanatory to anyone willing to recognize what is going on in athletics in these places presumably under *educational* sponsorship.

This most unfortunate development throughout the 20th century is only symptomatic of the entire society, however. My position about this aspect of society is basically this: "Sport was created by humans presumably to serve humans beneficially". As it is now, many semi-professional and professional athletes--not to mention the situation in much overly emphasized high school sport competition--are there to serve the whims of what has become a highly undesirable "sport goliath with an insatiable appetite for 'athletic peons'." This type of sport is fostered by a mindless public watching with vicarious, often rapturous involvement in a way akin to the seduction of the populace that occurred in ancient Rome. While this is taking place, the overwhelming majority of children and young people throughout the country are getting an inadequate introduction (or none at all!) to what ought to be a fine program of physical activity & health education and physical recreation in the public schools and related institutions. *I believe this is a most serious problem that must be addressed!*

The aggressive effort to export American "values" and the deplorable situation in commercialized competitive sport represent just the tip of the iceberg in the overall disintegrating situation that has developed. I can mention the rapid expansion of kiddy pornography, the ongoing exposes of illegal stock market manipulation, and the sex scandals that have devastated confidence in the Catholic clergy especially. Prurient sex increasingly clutters television along with inane programming with no intrinsic value. The violence of the ever-present video games is almost matched by the violence just about everywhere on the television channels.

These problems are bad enough, but what about the loss of several generations of Blacks in the United States, both men and women, through failure of the government to solve the problems of the inner cities. Just check out the number of Blacks (men only?) warehoused in prisons in 2000 as opposed to the total 20 years previously. The number has doubled from 400,000 to at least 800,000. Recently it was reported that 600,000 prisoners were being returned to society this year. What will this mean to our "way of life?" Still further, we've got another "type" of homeless cluttering up the cities, people who have often been turned out of inadequate "mental" institutions even though often unable to fend for themselves adequately.

These problems enumerated above are just the beginning of an almost endless list that demonstrates how the value structure is crumbling. The "rich are getting infinitely richer than the poor," and you know the remaining words of this statement. Ecology and economic capitalism are clashing anywhere and everywhere one chances to look in the world. See Michael Moore's insightful film "The Corporation" for detailed documentation of this assertion.

Freedom of speech is being trampled by the authorities because of suspected terrorist activity. The presumed leadership role of the United Nations is not being realized because of rising nationalism. The clash of cultures hypothesized by Toynbee at mid-20th century, and then re-emphasized by Huntington in the 1990's, is becoming a reality. Hard-won rights for union workers are being challenged on all fronts because "conditions demand it", they say. Hence it is becoming increasingly difficult to reach and maintain firm agreements that will help many millions of people to achieve so-called middle-class status..

Multiculturalism is literally being forced on many countries by legal and illegal immigrants, many of which are unwilling to accept the mores and accompanying culture of the land to which they immigrated. Vital population control is fought vigorously by established religious institutions determined to spread their message at any cost while they market additional converts. Lotteries are rampant, tempting semi-impoverished people to take money away from subsistence items they need. Condos that soon leak are planned, built, and inspected inadequately. This listing could continue almost indefinitely.

To return briefly to the realm of what is called sport, we find farcical professional wrestling, barbaric mixed "martial arts", burgeoning sport gambling, and consumption of illegal drugs to achieve unearned status in competitive sport at all levels. As mentioned above, even "respectable" universities have sold their heritage for a mess of pottage as they permit athletes to flaunt academic standards. At the same time the average youngster gets no, or probably inadequate, health education, physical activity education, and safety education at all levels of education.

An "Ethics Gap" Exists

In *A Way Out of Ethical Confusion* (Trafford, 2004), I sought to explain more briefly and succinctly than in *Who Knows What's Right Anymore?* (Trafford, 2002), how all of this came about, how and why such a terrible "ethics gap" exists. Where previously, for many at least, at least a relatively strong, orthodox, religious indoctrination prevailed. Today I feel such indoctrination as exists for the relatively few deeply involved (*actually!*) is most inadequate and is steadily declining as well. This is not necessarily a bad thing in one respect, because these institutions have not kept up with the times because of the "built-in" rigidity of their doctrines. (Yet if they don't adjust, they should be replaced!) In sum, the situation has steadily deteriorated in our present multi-ethnic, secular culture to a point where "confusion reigns" as to what constitutes ethical conduct.

It just so happens that I taught for 50 plus years, and I have been writing articles and books for 72 years. Early on I found that I was especially interested in the subject of values and accompanying norms. (As used here a "value" means a "principle" or "standard," while a "norm" is a "pattern of societal behavior" based on an established principle or standard [i.e., a value].) So for teaching purposes, as well as for my own personal ones, and my writing purposes, I developed the three self-evaluation checklists included here as appendices. One is titled "What Do I Believe?", a philosophical checklist that is included as an appendix. Another is called "Where Are You On a Socio-Political Spectrum?" It comprises a second appendix. The third is titled "How Do You Rate Yourself Recreationally?" Here one assesses how much he/she is "getting out of life." The basic assumption in each of these self-evaluation devices is that, to be logical in your approach to life, you need to know first where you stand as to your basic values. The three of these together are designed to "fortify" a person as he or she seeks to "live life" happily, meaningfully, and successfully in a democratic society in a free world..

Hence, at this point in my "Natterings", it seemed to be the proper time to review my own philosophic beliefs, as well as aspects of my socio-political stance as they relate to ongoing issues and problems of the day. In addition, I will explain a bit about my recreational "RQ" This was the third self-evaluation technique that I developed originally for use with my students in a professional-preparation program leading to a life typically as a professional educator. (Periodically I updated all three of them.) I found these "devices" to be very helpful and useful myself, and I discovered subsequently that they were helpful to several generations of undergraduate and graduate students as well. My reasoning in this regard was simply this: If these soon-to-be teacher/coaches don't "understand themselves," how can they possibly help *their* students later on to be effective teachers and managers of physical activity education and competitive sport.

My Personal Philosophic Beliefs

As far my personal, philosophical beliefs are concerned, I reviewed (1) the nature of reality (metaphysics), (2) ethics (axiology), (3) educational aims and objectives, and (4) the learning process (so-called epistemology. In the process I can say that I am still "a progressive, a liberal, and a pragmatist" in the full sense of these terms. What this adds up to under four appropriate categories (used for determination) is in the following paragraphs.

The Nature of Reality (Metaphysics). As I look at nature, there appears to be what is called "emerging evolution" taking place. As humans, this frame of reality we enjoy is limited as it functions. Everywhere I look our world is characterized by activity and change. Humans have developed what we call "rationality" over millions of years in this evolving situation, and there doesn't seem t be an end in sight in this incomplete world. In addition, a theory of "emergent novelty" appears to be operating within the universe. People enjoy true freedom of will that they can achieve by continuous and developmental learning from experience.

Ethics (Axiology). My belief here is that there should be no distinction between moral goods and natural goods. In other words the facts/values dualism that has been in existence should be eradicated as soon as possible by the use of scientific method applied to ethical situations. This means that we should employ reflective thinking to obtain the ideas that will function as tentative solutions for the solving of life's concrete problems. These ideas can then serve as hypotheses to be tested in life experimentally. If the ideas work in solving problematic situations, they become true. In this way we are able to use empirical verification of hypotheses that will over time bring theory and practice into a closer union. When we achieve agreement in factual belief, agreement in attitudes about this subject should soon follow. In this way science can ultimately bring about complete agreement on factual belief or knowledge about human behavior. The result of this approach is simply that there will be a continuous adaptation of values to the culture's changing needs. This in turn will effect the directed reconstruction of all social institutions.

Educational Aims and Objectives. The general aim of education is more education. Education in the broadest sense can be nothing else than the changes made in human beings by their experience. Participation by students in the formation of aims and objectives is absolutely essential to generate the all-important desired interest required for the finest educational process to occur. In addition, social efficiency (i.e., societal socialization) can well be considered the general aim of education. With this approach, pupil growth is a paramount goal. *This means that the individual is placed at the center of the educational experience, not the transmission of facts and knowledge to the learner.*

The Educative Process (Epistemeology) Knowledge is acquired by a person as a result of a process of thought with a useful purpose. Hence, truth is not only to be tested by its correspondence with reality, but also by its practical results. We "earn" knowledge through experience and it becomes an instrument of verification. What we call "mind" is not something separate from "body". It has evolved in the natural order of things as a more flexible means whereby people can adapt themselves to the world. We can say that learning takes place when interest and effort unite to produce the desired result. A psychological order of learning (problem-solving as explained through scientific method) is ultimately more useful (productive?) than a logical arrangement (proceeding from the simple fact to the complex conclusion). However, we shouldn't forget that there is always a social context to learning, and the curriculum itself should be adapted to the particular society for which it is intended.

My Socio-Political Stance

Next I will review where I stand (i.e., scored) on the socio-political evaluation test that I created some 50 years ago and have periodically updated since then because of changing times. On this self-evaluation device I amassed some 17 socio-political categories and then aligned them as carefully as possible "from left to right" on what I call a socio-political spectrum (i.e., from -51 on the left to +51 on the right in steps of 3 points for "movement" either to the right or left. In other words a person scoring a total of -51 would have been the most "liberal" in the position that he/she took on all 17 topics included in this assessment. Conversely, a score of -51 for a person would mean that this individual took "the farthest right" position on all 17 controversial socio-political issues. My personal score, as I assessed the many questions was consistently a "solid -2", thus my overall total was -34, and I could reasonably accurately call myself a "solid" or "confirmed" liberal or progressive.

The following, therefore, as my "confirmed" beliefs about these 17 socio-political issues or problems:

Issue #1. The place of the United Nations in world government should be expanded , and it should be involved with the actual enforcement of peacekeeping.

Issue #2. The world should provide aid to developing nations to the best of its ability, but only to those who ask for such aid and are willing to use it for sound economic development. The channeling of aid through an international agency is basic.

Issue #3. Countries should intervene militarily in the affairs of another country only when required (by United Nations and NATO) at a time when the need is extreme. Such "interference" should be only in an effort to bring peace and to protect further loss of life. In the future, major powers should gradually disarm to an "irreducible minimum."

Issue #4. In a hostage crisis where one country holds one country holds another country's citizens at ransom (or for whatever purpose), such action warrants the following action: There should be a protest through diplomatic channels for an explanation with a plea for swift action and the safety of the hostages.

Issue #5. Youth, both at home and abroad, are causing considerable concern to governmental officials at all levels. I feel that young people are often justified in their struggle to change the basic nature of the society. Ethnic minority groups, Blacks (in the States), and young people should not have to wait forever for much-needed change. Many fundamental institutions must be rebuilt from the ground up. (What they should do about it is another question, however…)

Issue #6, Public welfare programs in North America are urgently needed and should be coordinated by the federal government. There should be a minimum, guaranteed annual income for all needy families sufficient to provide a reasonable standard of living pro-rated to the cost-of-living in the geographical region involved. Billions are needed as soon as possible to upgrade all aspects of the lives of the poor and neglected members of society.

Issue #7. The rights of freedom of speech and press contained, for example, in the First Amendment of the U.S. Constitution, are perhaps the most important rights granted to citizens by government in constitutions and bills of right. Movements to dilute or "balance away" these rights in the interest of national security have typically been misdirected. Suppression of speech and movement should be carried out only in most extreme situations.

Issue #8. Laissez faire capitalism certainly helped this country initially to become strong materially. Now, however, the rich are getting richer, and the poor are "vice versa". We obviously need somewhat more of a social-welfare state approach to meet the urgent needs of a significant percentage of the people.

Issue #9. Law and order is absolutely necessary in a democratic society, but the words as used by many take on an unpleasant overtone. Crimes rates of several types are really serious, but we must move positively rather than negatively to reach their causes and then correct them. Prison rehabilitation programs must be improved significantly. I believe that crime rates would go down markedly if competency-based education and more jobs were made available.

Issue #10. The population control situation is starkly grim today. It has become now become so tragic because there are more than seven billion people on earth--and the projection figure is nine billion before a declining trend is expected. We are told that all-out cooperative efforts by the major powers in the world simply cannot ward off the massive starvation of peoples that is coming in the years ahead.

Issue #11. The union movement for middle- and lower-class workers gives me hope that the world can be a fair place in which to live. Unions have given workers a sense of security and morale that permits them to work more productively and comfortably at the same time.

Issue #12. Competitive sport was created by people thousands of years ago (presumably) to serve humankind beneficially. It can and does serve a multitude of purposes in today's world. With sound leadership it can be good for both boys and girls in their formative years. It can help to develop desirable character and personality traits and also promote vigorous health. It can also provide good role models for young people to emulate. Our states and provinces should get fully behind these activities by providing appropriate competition for all young people as they are developing. Such sporting competition should be regarded as supplemental to regular physical activity education programs at all levels of education.

Issue #13. *The New York Times* reported, for example, "our morality is disintegrating because its foundation is eroding." The Washington Post asserted: "The core of U.S. national character has been damaged because we've lost our sense of virtue!" I find myself essentially in agreement with the position taken immediately above by the writer. Times are indeed changing, and we simply must be fair to *all* concerned. A number of the concerns expressed about gay and lesbian relationships are not central to "the good life"--they are peripheral. What is important in life is that we should be fair, decent, and just in our relationships with others--not that we should concern ourselves with people's sexual preferences. A spectrum seems to exist about the "maleness" or "femaleness" of a person, a condition that is inherent in that individual and cannot be altered without maladjustment occurring.

Issue #14. It has been stated that the overwhelming magnitude of poor ecological practices has not been even partially understood by the general populace. Now some realize the urgency of the matter, but others are telling them that further study is needed, that the ecologists are exaggerating, and that they are simply pessimistic by nature. I find myself in essential agreement that this is a crisis. The need for "ecological awareness" is racing headlong into a collision with growing worldwide capitalism in the burgeoning global economy. The time is now to take drastic steps to alleviate and/or resolve this overwhelmingly difficult problem.

Issue #15. In the 21st century, castigating scientists for "staggering arrogance" in presuming to play God by conducting cloning research does not cut much ice with me. (Note that god is spelled with a capital "G.") As humankind seeks "what is possible", we must also ask what is right--and we must not forget that "even the most noble ends do not justify any means". The question is whether such investigation will result in a better future for humankind.

Unless knowledge of "how it all began" somehow becomes known to humankind–and can we really believe this will ever happen? --we earthlings do not have much choice. We must figure out--working together! --what's "right" action and what's "wrong" action for us in the 21st century. Our decisions quite simply must be based on our own life experience. If we do not manage to do this, ultimate disaster to life as we know it today seems almost inevitable. Findings from the scientific community about "how to live" keep flooding in. Some ideas are good, some debatable, and some turn out to be wrong. Life moves on in often strange and mysterious ways. It appears to be an open-ended universe. We do not really know where we came from, or where we are going. Scientific discoveries and the medical profession backed by the health sciences have lengthened the average length of human life. Now we are promised even better length and longevity through cellular research. I say, "Go for it!"

Issue #16. So-called "universal health care" is now a great problem for countries of the world to solve. This is so because the expense of paying for all sorts of medical expenses, including some based on incomplete scientific backing, has become prohibitive. To pay for everything "eats up" a "disproportionatc" amount of as country's overall budget.

In North America, for example, the United States has a situation in which some 45% of the population has no governmental medical coverage. In addition, it is not known what percentage of the remainder have policies that provide that could be termed "inadequate" coverage. Often when a specific claim is made, the response is that either coverage is not available on the existing policy, or that only a percentage of the needed amount will be paid.

Everything considered, in the 21st country a North American country ought to provide full medical coverage for all of its citizens regardless of their ability to pay. Not to do so creates a situation in which the needs of rich people are met in one way or another, The needs of the middle-class may be met, but some times by incurring long term-debt. In addition, the poor simply "fade away" and die sooner. The only fair and just conclusion is that the total expense should be borne by the government through its taxation scheme.

Issue #17. The general aim of education is more education. Education in the broadest sense can be nothing else than the changes made in human beings by their experience. Participation by students in the formation of aims and objectives is essential to generate the all-important desired interest required for the finest educational process to occur. Social efficiency (i.e., societal socialization) should be considered the general aim of education. Pupil growth is a paramount goal. This means that the individual is placed at the center of the educational experience.

My Recreational Quotient ("RQ")

After discovering through my "personal updating" that my "stances" or "positions" in regard to both philosophic outlook and socio-political stance were essentially the same. I moved next to assess what I years ago designated as a person's "recreational quotient" or "RQ". Somehow although and members of my family had always led very busy lives, we had always managed to enrich our lives individually and collectively through involvement with a variety of recreational/educational activities. The self-evaluation text I devised was titled: "Whatever Happened to :The Good Life?" (or Assessing Your "RQ" (Recreation Quotient).

The term "recreation" seems to have gradually but steadily developed a broader meaning. Typically, recreation embodies those experiences or activities that people have or engage in during their leisure for the purpose of pleasure, satisfaction, or education. Recreation is, therefore, a human experience or activity; it is not necessarily instinctive; and it may be considered as purposeful—but not for its survival value.

I reasoned, therefore, that one's "RQ" or Recreation Quotient, is the sum or total of individual recreational experiences a person is having regularly in activities available under each of the five broad categories of recreation available to humans (i.e., sport & physical recreation interests, social recreation interests, communicative recreation interests, esthetic & creative recreation interests, and "learning" recreation interests [e.g., hobbies]).

The test itself is based on a scale moving from passive, to vicarious, to active, to creative involvement in life's educational and recreational activities. It gives you more credit if you are a most interested onlooker or listener rather than a passive one. Moreover, you will score even higher if you actively take part in a particular recreational activity. The highest rating goes to the person who participates in a superior and/or creative fashion.

When I first developed this test for use with my students, I was about 30 years old, Hence, as I am writing these words today, I wondered how much change there would be in my final tally today as opposed to the first time I took it. When I rated myself in the five categories involved some 55 years ago, I discovered that my total score (out of a possible total of 50 points-i.e., scoring 10 in each of five categories) was 36 points. Interestingly-to me anyhow-my score 56 years later is 35 pts.

However, I am quick to point out that I "earned" my points then *differently* because my physical attributes and interests have changed. For example, I earned 10 points in the Sports and Physical Activity Column "back then" by playing handball and/or or paddle ball three times a week. Now I earned 10 pts., also, but I did so by lap swimming three times a week at a set pace and distance. Another example would be the 4 points ((1 and 3, respectively) that I earned under "Social Activities" now, as opposed to the 10 pts. I earned in 1955.

Hence, all together I now score a total of 35 pts. overall for the five categories, whereas "back then" I was somehow closed to 5o pts.! Intcresting! To me anyhow…

Your Personal Philosophic Beliefs

"What Do I Believe?" Now I ask you, my reader, to find yourself on the philosophical spectrum in regard to your basic beliefs about life and living. Next I ask you to discover your socio-political stance or position. Third, and finally, I ask you to determine your score on the recreation self-evaluation questionnaire ("RQ") (See appendices.)

The reason I asked you to look deeply inside yourself to perhaps re-discover your basic values is simple and straightforward. What you discover here is absolutely fundamental. ***This is you!*** If you haven't done this previously, and/or if you don't do it now, you are living what the ancient philosopher (Plato) is purported to have said about lives such lived: "The unexamined life is not worth living!"

Your Socio-Political Stance

"Where Am I on a Socio-Political Spectrum?" Once you know, or re-affirm

where you stand in the "value department," you are ready for the questionnaire Appendix B. This should help you figure out where you stand on a socio-political spectrum--not where you may nominally have thought you were. When someone asks, "Where do you stand politically?" Or perhaps "Are you a member of a political party? What will you say now in response? Are you a conservative, a liberal, or a maverick? (A maverick, of course, is an independent or an "unbranded animal.") And, whatever you say, are you prepared to explain your position? Further, if not, why not? Could it be that you still haven't really thought it out carefully and fully? Or are you simply continuing with the political stance that you "inherited" from your parents? Or is the case that you will vote one way or the other just to keep peace with your girl friend or spouse? Basically, if you follow through and "locate yourself," do you now know *how* to justify your socio-political stance? *And if so, are you going to do anything about it?*

Whatever your answers to the above questions may are, you may have at least now spelled out where you stand based on the answers you gave to a series of graduated questions under three different categories of your life. Keep in mind that your responses do not necessarily equate with the presently stated platforms of existing political parties in either the United States or Canada. Frankly, I believe there is vast confusion out there in this regard--that is, vacillation depending on the changing times or simply misunderstanding or *not* understanding fully...

Some people will admit that they are radical or reactionary (i.e., far left or far right). It may be that you are neutral, or middle-of-the-road, it will be possible to make that determination based on your answers to this questionnaire. Why is this determination of socio-political "position" or "stance" important? Simply because a person with an "ordered mind" is able to state his/her beliefs and opinions with reasonable consistency based on a set of generally accepted values. *Reasoned thought should result in positive action.*

Your Recreational Quotient ("RQ")

"Assessing Your 'RQ' (Recreation Quotient)". In this evaluation device in this book's appendix, I offer you also a chance to assess your "RQ" or so-called "recreation quotient". I did this because I believe that we in North America were promised "the good life," but that such a state has not materialized for many millions of the citizenry. This is nothing new, of course. Throughout

history all societies have misused leisure after they struggled long and hard to earn it. In certain instances the misuse of free time has actually caused the downfall of that society.

Of course, one development in modern society has been that people are increasingly crowded together in heavily populated urban and suburban communities. This creates a problem: How can people find happiness, satisfaction, and a high quality of life despite and increased tempo of living and increasing crowded conditions? The test was based the test on a scale moving from passive, to vicarious, to active, to creative involvement in life's many educational/recreational activities. It gives the individual more credit if he or she is a most interested onlooker or listener rather than a passive one. Moreover, a person will score even higher if there is active involvement in a particular recreational activity. The highest rating goes to the person who participates in a superior and/or creative fashion.

North Americans have been accused of having "spectatoritis" (that is, spending too much of their free time watching others taking part in some form of activity or recreation). Many people are now concerned about whether they are getting sufficient pleasure out of life. So I developed this simple, self-evaluative test so that men and women of all ages could rate themselves recreationally and then take steps as they wish to improve their "recreational quotient" ("RQ"). There is no doubt but that sound recreational pursuits can add zest and vigor to our lives. However, there are many ways of looking at the subject of recreation.

The Missing Link: A Life Purpose

"Okay." "Enough already," you may be saying. "I have checked out my value system, what I believe. I'm a such-and-such. I know where I fall on the socio-political spectrum. I have even checked out my recreation quotient, and I'm perhaps not getting enough fun and pleasure out of life. Where do I go from here?"

I agree that this question is basic and vital. With all of the above results, whether conflicting or consonant with what you thought you were before getting involved, I found personally that there was a missing link. I discovered what I believed about the world and the people in it. I learned where I "was coming from" on the socio-political spectrum. Further I checked myself out as to recreation quotient, but there was still *a missing link*.

That missing link for me "way back then" was that I really didn't have a life purpose. *I needed to find one before I figured that I had made my life worth living.*

A long time ago, so long I don't like to think about it, there was a president of Columbia University by the name of Nicholas Murray Butler. This was back in the days when we didn't "batter" our leaders anywhere nearly like we do today. In one of his talks he said: "There are three kinds of people in the world: (1) those who make things happen; (2) a larger number who watch things happen; and (3) the vast majority who never even know that anything is going on." Of course, this is somewhat of an exaggeration. However, as I read about his remarks, I thought to myself: "Gee, I'd like to be one of those people who *make* things happen! This sounds trite, to be sure. It is a noble aim, of course. The words are easy to say, *but the goal of finding and achieving a life purpose is infinitely harder to accomplish.*

Nevertheless, regardless of whether one achieves this goal of a life purpose, striving for immediate objectives looking to a long-range aim is very important for anyone. Here I have argued that one needs to (1) determine his or her personal values; (2) place these values in some hierarchical order; (3) relate personal values as best possible to the values and norms of the North American culture within the prevailing world culture; (4) analyze one's own abilities and interests while ascertaining the needs and interests of the present era; and, finally, (5) to nurture a chosen life purpose *so that maximum energy for living results.*

Admittedly it has been very difficult for people to decide upon personal and societal values. The home and the church ran into serious difficulty during the second half of the 20th century coping with this problem--and the school and the university have been reluctant and therefore slow to fill this gap. Since the days of the ancient Greeks, savants have been plagued by the question of whether education should be both rational *and moral.* (Private schools try to do this, but the public ones quake in their boots over this dilemma.) Is a commitment to moral values taught or caught; do you teach about it; and do you teach a commitment to it?

Further, it is easy to confuse means and ends along the way toward the achievement of a set of personal values. For example, are the following means or ends--or both: sound health, religious faith, knowledge, truth, personal recognition, service to others, creativity, desirable personality traits, pleasure, and the capacity from a lifelong education in a democratic society?

Philosophy and "Sense of Life." For some unexplained reason we go at this most important aspect of our development in a typically haphazard manner. If a child has a mother and father who are able to spend a large amount of time with him or her, and these people are intelligent, sensitive, and dedicated to the task of raising a child, that young person is most fortunate indeed. This is true because it is during these formative years that a child's "sense of life" gets off to a good, bad, or indifferent beginning. The philosopher Ayn Rand, much maligned as she was—and occasionally deservedly so-discusses this stage of life most cogently in her *The Romantic Manifesto*. She explained her belief that religion offers a myth or allegory stating that there is a supernatural recorder from whom none of a human's deeds can be hidden. She stated, "That myth is true, not existentially, but psychologically. The merciless recorder is "the integrating mechanism of a man's [sic] sub-conscious; the record is his 'sense of life'"(1969, p. 31).

Because of the importance of Rand's thought on this matter, I will paraphrase her sequence of ideas. This sense of life is a pre–conceptual, subconsciously integrated appraisal of existence, man, and that person's emotional responses and character essence. Thus, before a person has a chance to study philosophy--if one ever does in today's world--he/she makes choices, forms value judgments, experiences emotions, and acquires an implicit view of life. If the person has the opportunity subsequently to develop his/her rational powers, the hope is generally that reason will act as the programmer of the individual's "emotional computer." and then the earlier sense of life may develop into a rational philosophy. If--for some reason--we don't know how, or don't make the effort, or never have the opportunity to understand that *we need to develop such rationality as the basis for the possible future emergence of a life purpose*, then chance takes over. The person then tends to become a machine without a driver that is (as Rand explains) 'integrating blindly, incongruously, and at random" (p. 33).

A hierarchy of values, whether implicitly or explicitly derived, tells what is important to a person. It serves as a bridge between the person's beliefs about the world and that individual's ethical system. "The integrated sum of a person's basic values is that person's sense of life" (p. 35). The goal is "a fully integrated personality, a man whose mind and emotions are in harmony; whose sense of life matches his convictions" (p. 36). This sense of life is his "automatically integrated sum of his values," but the hope is that thereafter the enlightened person will derive his/her value judgments conceptually (being derived from belief about the nature of the universe).

Relationship to Social Values. The relationship of one's implicit sense of life and/or explicit philosophy of life should, presumably, be reasonably consistent with the values and norms of the society in which that individual is functioning. If not, serious difficulties may arise (for that person at least). Proceeding on the assumption that the various subsystems of the general action system of a society together compose a hierarchy of control and conditioning, our cultural values (i.e., social, scientific, artistic, educational, sport values) determine the state of our culture in the long run *if* the action system is functioning properly. Our societal values in this evolving democratic society determine our so-called cultural pattern or configuration--i.e., the *programming* for the entire cultural action system.

In a classification of the fundamental values of the United States--an attempt to perceive the self-orientation in relation to the collectivity orientation--the United States is viewed as being more achievement oriented, universalistic, equalitarian, and self-oriented than, for example, Canada. However, the value differences were considered not that great at the beginning of the last quarter of the 20th century. These differences are probably due to "varying origins in their political systems, national identities, varying religious traditions, and varying frontier experiences" (Lipset in Koulack and Perlman, 1973: 4-5). Our problem as individuals is, therefore, that we as individuals must work within *our* system and its ascribed values. If we can't stand what we find there, we should work to change things--or possibly move elsewhere.

Questions Regarding a Life Purpose

At this point I come down "foursquare" on the need for a person to find a life purpose if he or she wants to reach full potential. After personal values have been consciously determined in relation to whatever implicit sense of life has developed, these values, explicit and implicit, should be related as best possible to the values and norms that prevail in the social system where one lives. This life purpose may be discovered by asking oneself such questions as:

> (1) What is it I want to do more than anything else in the world?
> (2) Will my chosen work give me the greatest amount of satisfaction?
> (3) Will I be able to follow through tentatively with my initial decision before making a final decision?

A life purpose should be much more than the mere choice of, and efforts to fulfill the demands of, a job or occupation. It involves even more than the choice *of*, and following through *with*, a profession. The meaning of the terms "profession" and "trade" seem to have blended into each other in the last half of the 20th century. Serving in the professions earlier (e.g., the law, the military, teaching, medicine) meant *service to humanity* was placed before personal gain. Granted that selecting a profession or a trade is a means to an end. We must ask what that *end,* that goal is. When we talk about a life purpose, the term *vocation* would be better. A vocation, if we keep the word's Latin derivation in mind, is a *calling*.

Using the word "calling" to describe where one's life purpose can be found, we encounter immediately the idea of accomplishing something of significance for the total movement of life on this planet. I am pragmatic enough to believe that this idea has validity even today despite the turmoil and despair evident all around us. This take-what-you-find-and improve-it approach to life is called *philosophical meliorism*. It equates nicely with Berelson and Steiner's "behavioral-science image" of man and woman recommended in the "dark days" of the 1960's (1964, pp. 662-667). They equated a human as a creature who is continually and continuously adapting reality to his or her own ends. Within this context a person should inquire as to what kind of striving gives life its greatest meaning. (However, keep in mind that sacrificing oneself for some cause with no thought of finding g enjoyment in the effort would not seem to be the best approach. To effect the most fruitful results from your labor, I believe you must be enjoying yourself--even if through vicarious satisfaction.)

As a person searches for a life purpose, the following steps may be useful:

(1) Thinking reflectively,
(2) Observing and asking questions of others,
(3) Enacting a process of self-measurement and evaluation,
(4) Ascertaining the needs and opportunities of the time, and
(5) Listening to the thoughts of close relatives, friends, and associates.

Nurturing a Life Purpose

After finding a life purpose, or at least initially accepting some plan, it must be nurtured for effective development. We are actually confronted with a "move it or lose it" ultimatum. It should be talked through, and possibly even written out. Such a statement should be revised yearly, because a life purpose ought to grow. A person should rededicate himself/herself anew from time to time. A purpose may change or alter somewhat, of course, but it should be fostered by the development of a strong personal attitude (psychologically speaking!) that will help the individual to avoid any gradual surrendering to the shifting currents present in the onrushing, ever-changing society.

A person will often find it difficult to hold true to the vocation that is chosen. This is more difficult for women than for men, because they are the ones who bear the children. The purpose may have to be guarded against a variety of "ills" that may appear from time to time. Other career opportunities may present themselves that will hold out greater material reward or more rapid success. It is true that success comes more quickly for some than it does for others. Further, there will be ways to make more money that will in time detract from the accomplishment of the avowed life purpose. Youth may be long gone before years of dedicated efforts in certain professions bring what society terms as success. In some cases recognition comes only after a person's death. I can't prove this statement to you, but I believe it quite probable that the course of human history has been shaped by personalities who have held to high purposes over a long period of years on behalf of humankind.

As we "nurture a life purpose," we must guard that the means do not become confused with the end--that we don't get bogged down with life's "instrumentalities." By that I mean that so many people seem to spend time getting ready to live that they never quite get around to living itself. Further, I am personally convinced that much of the joy should come from "traveling hopefully along the way"! This coincides to a degree with the oft-heard homily: "Enjoy yourself; it's later than you think..."

In achieving this life purpose I have been describing, the search is for what the ancient Greek philosopher, Aristotle, called "the golden mean." We shouldn't become fanatics or egomaniacs; yet, ordinary expenditure of effort and/or lackadaisical apathy won't bring expected results. A person can't ignore the conditions that must be met to fulfill a life purpose. Yet, he or she shouldn't ignore the important interests of humankind. The task--truly a delicate problem involving careful delineation--is to be sufficiently passionate about one's purpose in life while avoiding the sad and irritating (to others!) pitfall of fanaticism.

Particularly important in achieving this delicate balance--this difficult golden mean that will allow one to achieve his/her life purpose--is the attainment of a battery of knowledge, competencies, skills, attitudes, and conditions. In this age of specialization, *knowledge* equates with power; *competencies* are needed to meet both the general and specific demands of life; *skills* are required to solve the problems of varying complexity faced each day (not to forget what Postman and Weingartner earlier titled "crap-detecting" ability); *attitudes* are needed that exhibit care and concern for humanity--love for humanity everywhere; and a *condition* (i.e. a state of health) that provides the vigor and endurance needed to accomplish one's chosen life purpose.

A "Formula for Happiness and Success"

What then might be a "formula" for happiness and success? In offering a list of "ingredients," admittedly normative and unscientific, no effort has been made to present the eight aspects of the formula in any hierarchical order. My position is simply that the ingredients of this formula, applied to the degree or extent that must be personally determined, will enable a person to reach his or her goals in life--i.e., achieve a chosen life purpose. Achieving these objectives will cumulatively contribute to the long-range aim of "happiness" and "success" in life. My belief is that a competency (i.e., an adequacy or sufficiency) in each of the seven aspects is possible. Achieving a life purpose will require passionate and purposeful fulfillment of these specific objectives:

(1) Desirable personality and character traits (which are presumably the result of nature, nurture, and other unplanned experiences).
(2) Successful human relations (which involve the home and other social groups).
(3) A broadly based general education in the humanities, social sciences, and natural sciences.
(4) An intensive, specialized professional preparation (which should prepare the individual for the highest type of position

available in accordance with one's potential).

(5) Regular, active physical recreation and exercise involvement (which should achieve continuing physical fitness and enjoyable, recreational play).

(6) Creative educational/recreational participation (that may be carried out to a desired degree in social, communicative, esthetic and creative, and "learning" recreational interests).

Fulfillment of these objectives to the extent required for a desired "amalgam" should enable a person to achieve a desired life purpose. Such a long-range goal should be pursued passionately but not fanatically.

This, then, is what I believe a person should consider as he/she looks forward to the development of a life purpose in a chosen field of endeavor. At the same time the "prescription" includes ingredients that can well lead to the elusive goals of happiness and success however defined. I repeat that a life purpose should be pursued passionately for maximum effectiveness. For the best type--the highest type--of professional involvement, a person must "lose" himself/herself in service to humanity with minimum concern for a high level of monetary return. Satisfaction, recognition, and other rewards will not come rapidly with this approach. They will come nevertheless toward the end of a long life of service, as well as through the improvement and gratitude of those for whom you expend such energy and effort.

Finally, the words of the late Bertrand Russell, the eminent British philosopher, still offer us sound advice as we look to the future:

> I wanted on the one hand to find out whether anything could be known; and, on the other hand, to do whatever might be possible toward creating what might be a happier world . . . as I have grown older, my optimism has grown more sober and the happy issue more distant . . . The causes of unhappiness in the past and in the present are not difficult to ascertain. There have been wars, oppressions, and tortures which have been due to men's hostility to their fellow men. And there have been morbid miseries fostered by gloomy creeds, which have led men into profound inner discord . . . I may have thought the road to a world of free and happy human beings shorter than it is proving to be, but I was not wrong in thinking

that such a world is possible, and that it is worthwhile to
live with a view to bringing it nearer. I have lived in the
pursuit of such a vision, both personal and social . . .
These things I believe, and the world, for all its horrors,
has left me unshaken (1969, Vol. 3, pp. 318 et ff.)

Although we may all wish that peace, happiness, harmony, and well-being could prevail globally, such has not yet happened. One is inclined to hope that all of the clashing religious opinions and beliefs based on hoary tradition would silently go away. Then maybe prevailing world conditions would somehow improve. But this is wishful thinking unless improved institutions are created to take their place and make the entire world a better place in which to live.

Our task as individuals, through full commitment to a life purpose, is to contribute to the achievement of a world of free, happy, and healthy human beings. In this way we have the opportunity to join the tradition laid down by those enlightened people who preceded us. "Man errs, but strive he must!" (Goethe)

Selection 4
Accepting Liberalism for Guidance in Life

Keeping in mind, therefore, (1) my attempt to interpret history philosophically, and (2) my subsequent thought that we "earthpeople" are best advised to look upon what we call "civilization" as an "adventure", next I discussed how I went about finding a life purpose. Naturally it occurred to me that I could use the approach I followed in connection with my work with undergraduate and graduate students. Right away I recognized that I had to be very careful not to seek to automatically "superimpose" my beliefs and "positions" on my students. Although I understand that the many public and private educational systems around the world had no compunctions about deciding what should be taught to students and how it should be taught, my personal belief and accompanying stance could never function in that fashion.

All indications pointed up the fact that I had become what is called a "liberal." Nevertheless, I confess up front that I have found discussion on the subject of what is called "liberalism" very confusing. I presume this is because the term has been used *and* in addition how "abused" from different directions over the course of recent centuries. Of course, it is used quite a bit in society when complaints are lodged about "academe", but not as frequently as conservatives charge. It is used, also, by the average citizen to describe a "left-leaning" person ("a liberal!") or the political stance that person might hold in everyday politics.

Although early in my life, members of both sides of my divided family were strongly conservative both politically and religiously, I somehow ended up as a confirmed *liberal*. (That's a "small l" liberal, although I can say that I have earlier on occasion voted for the Liberal party in Canada as well.) So, because of the term's "omnipresence" within several circles of society, I felt it necessary to ascertain to what extent my own position was consonant to what is typically regarded as "being a liberal".

I was interested, also, to see what implications acceptance or rejection of this position, either socially or politically, might have on education generally. Then, specifically, because I ended up with a doctoral degree in the history and philosophy of education, I wanted to learn whether the acceptance or rejection of this stance might have any influence on the type of educational program, including the physical activity education (and sport) aspect that would be promoted by such a person for himself/herself and for society.

Classical Liberals, *Modern* Liberals, etc.

We read that there are *classical* liberals (e.g., the philosopher John Locke) and *modern* liberals (e.g., a percentage of the totality of university professors). The late political scientist, David Spitz (*The Real World of Liberalism*, 1982), who investigated the topic thoroughly, explained that liberalism exists as a political ideology, but at times it is also used as a justification for an approach to economic theory. Further, in the discipline of philosophy, liberals are known as those who challenge ultimate truth or verities. Liberals are additionally at least somewhat hopeful about the intrinsic nature of humans and the possibility of human progress.

Therefore, believing that I was definitely "inclined" in the direction of liberalism, as opposed to conservatism, I was challenged seriously when one of my favorite philosophers, John Kekes, published his *Against Liberalism* in 1997. Explaining that the positive aim of liberals is to create a situation in which people can live "the good life," he asserts that creation of such values for *all* people *fully* would actually produce finally the evils liberals seek to avoid. In turn, subsequent attempts to reduce these evils would result in a lessening of any achievement of the liberal values sought. In addition, I became somewhat more disturbed when I read that Larry Gerber in *The Limits of Liberalism*, (1984) had pointed out that although liberal ideology had "inspired" many Americans in the 20th century, he believed that it had left many Americans with a "dubious legacy" (Chap. IX, pp. 341-349).

Still further, John Stuhr (*Pragmatism, Postmodernism, and the Future of Philosophy*, 2003) once again outlined the oft-repeated "evils" of liberalism as declared by the early 20th century philosopher W.E. Hocking. By using phrases like "incapable of achieving and maintaining political units," "attachment to rights without [accompanying] duties," and the emotional appeal of a doctrine that has a "cheerful, amiable view of human nature" (pp. 35-36), I found these criticisms sending me back to the proverbial drawing board. I won't repeat Hocking's proposed "essentialistic" (as opposed to "progressivistic") remedy for these foreseen evils, but at this point I could only counter with my long-term, considered agreement with John Dewey's position that liberalism would work if only society could muster a greater commitment to such a stance and to accompanying "democracy in action" within our political units.

Background and Status of the Term

With the increasing emphasis these days on being able to get a job and earn a living, the emphasis on enrollment in higher education in a degree program that will be of direct help in this direction, it does indeed appear that the emphasis of a broadly based liberal arts and science program declined in the second half of the twentieth century. North Americans should decide to what extent the traditional conception of a *liberal* education still holds meaning and should apply strongly in the 21st century. I repeat this, because at present we do indeed find this concept being downgraded as material demands loom larger in the minds of young people facing an indeterminate future seemingly more than ever before.

This concept of a 'liberal education' presumably came originally from ancient Greece, but underwent successive modifications during the periods of the Roman Empire, the medieval Church, the Renaissance, and the Reformation. There was a gradual evolution of a prescribed curriculum that became a "necessary prerequisite" for the bachelor of arts degree, the traditional mark of a liberally educated person.

As the Greeks lost their political liberty to Rome, the educated Greek was no longer a "man of action." Political expediency had actually forced him to become contemplative. Much later, when Rome had eventually fallen, at the beginning of the Middle Ages the liberal arts had been formalized and condensed from the broader Greek heritage into small literary packets of knowledge suitable only to intellectual and "spiritual" affairs. "Material life" was largely excluded from consideration.

With the advent of Scholasticism and the medieval universities, the liberal arts curriculum was again expanded. Specialization grew in the form of the studies of law, medicine, theology, and philosophy. The idea of a prescribed curriculum was basic, because the Church wanted clergymen and teachers to be orthodox in every respect.

The Renaissance added the study of classical civilization to the prescribed studies. It was at this time that secularism made an inroad into the traditional curriculum. The union of the "knightly" and the "humanistic" in the court schools of Italy was characterized by a training in arms and letters, both of which held places of distinction in the higher education of the time. Subsequently, the Reformation, with its emphasis on teaching people to read the vernacular, struck a vital blow in favor of the trend toward somewhat more democratic education.

The struggle between "culture" and "utility" has subsequently characterized curriculum development to the present day. Most educators will agree that it would be appropriate ethically for every child to achieve his or her optimum development. In the United States, for example, each child is promised "that all men are created equal; that they are endowed with certain inalienable rights; that among these are life, liberty, liberty, and the pursuit of happiness." The unfortunate reality is that world peace and an unlimited economic surplus are necessary to achieve this ideal state of affairs.

At mid-20th century, the United States was still seeking to lead the Western world in a type of sociological experiment to determine whether the concept of "life, liberty, and the pursuit of happiness" was to prevail over Communistic ideology. This experiment was successful in that the former Union of Soviet Socialistic Republics was broken up. However, China and certain other countries have retained Communistic ideology while adapting to the global economy with its capitalistic roots.

The traditional purpose of a liberal arts education was viewed typically as the development of an ability to analyze and discriminate value. However, it is my belief that such an aim is not being met sufficiently today in the face of educational experiences focused more on vocational development. It is argued that traditional liberal arts education is discriminatory in that it appears to be an "aristocratic pattern of education" for the intellectually elite members of society. Of course, any successful attempt at a democratic way of life makes necessary universal education for all. Within such a universal education pattern, all people should therefore be able to analyze and discriminate value successfully.

In the area of general education, the overall function should be to educate the individual as an enlightened person and as a cultured citizen in an evolving democracy. To become specific, *one problem to be met* by the student would be to participate in the social, economic, and political life of his/her community, state, nation, and world. A *selected competency* needed by this student to meet the requirement of one aspect of this problem would be the need to appreciate and foster the rights and responsibilities of the various racial and religious groups. The student should therefore have *a selected experience* whereby he/she would have an opportunity to attack discrimination and to work for the elimination of unfair practice. In this respect, then, several courses in the social sciences would serve as *resource areas* for the resolution of *the problem to be solved*. If such a *problem-solving approach* were used in general education, it could also be used effectively in professional education, as well as in liberal arts education. (The sciences do very nicely with problem-solving experiences, of course.)

Immediate Objectives; Long Range Aims?

The long-range aim in the face of so many demands on the educational curriculum in North America should presumably be a unification of liberal, vocational, and "avocational" education. Each of these elements (e.g., a liberal studies curriculum) should involve programs and accompanying courses that are all *competency-based*. Finally, prior to graduation, an overall, competency-based evaluation should take place before diplomas and degrees are awarded. *However, such **a** broadly based evaluation **b**ased on the assessment of necessary knowledge, competencies, and skills does not appear to be taking place anywhere nearly universally at present.*

John Dewey's Educational Goal

In a true democracy every person should eventually make a social return for his or her endeavor to be respected. Work should never be thought of as being disagreeable. If people are shown *why* they work, and *how* their efforts fit into the pattern of a "global village," the educational goal of John Dewey would be largely achieved. His vision was for an "inspiring vocational education with a liberal spirit and filled with a liberal content."

Today as perhaps never before, I believe that higher education in North America needs greater unity of purpose. The educational system should provide citizens with the means for ongoing survival. Such an education should be geared to the pursuit of excellence while at the same time preserving individual freedom. I firmly believe that the democratic way of life offers the best promise yet for a brighter future on planet Earth.

Unification of Liberal, Vocational, and "Avocational" Education

Finally, the objective in the face of so many demands on the core curriculum should be a unification of liberal, vocational, and "avocational" education. Each of these elements (e.g., liberal studies) should involve programs and accompanying courses that are all competency-based. *An overall, competency-based evaluation should take place before diplomas and degrees are awarded.*

In a true democracy every person should make a social return for his or her endeavor to be respected. Work should never be thought of as being disagreeable. If people are shown *why* they work, and *how* their efforts fit into the pattern of a "global village," the educational goal of John Dewey will be largely achieved. His vision was for an "inspiring vocational education with a liberal spirit and filled with a liberal content."

Today as perhaps never before, higher education in North America needs greater unity of purpose. The educational system must provide citizens with the means for ongoing survival. Such an education should be geared to the pursuit of excellence while at the same time preserving individual freedom. The democratic way of life offers the best promise yet for a brighter future on planet Earth.

The Influence of the "Aging Process"

As one gets older, there is a tendency to become overwhelmed with daily accounts of the world's evils and woes. Conservatives continue with their claims that intellectually elite professors on campuses use their classes to promote left-wing liberalism, socialism, relativistic ethics, and annoying political correctness. Faced with such damning, ongoing criticism, it is indeed so difficult to be optimistic about the future of higher education. This is especially so, because higher education has had to "look in many different directions" for the funding necessary for both survival and progress. Yet, it occurred to me that, if we stop to think about it, giving in to a *pessimistic* outlook regarding the promotion of "a liberal education for all" may indeed lead toward that state of affairs that we envision thereby. Conversely, I agree that the optimism of a Mary Poppins does indeed offers a bit too much of a "pie-in-the-sky" outlook for me. So what does one do? Neither the nay-saying pessimist nor the cheerful optimist makes a welcome bedfellow for me as society moves along into the twentieth-first century.

Meliorism: A "Middle" Position (?)

I have finally opted for a middle position between the two extremes. It is known as *philosophical meliorism*. It's a term that we don't hear very often, but it's actually one that represents a choice that we face every day of our lives. This means simply that a person should take the prevailing situation as he or she finds it--*and then work to make it better*! I decided to accept such a *melioristic* approach as a working model. I do recognize the perceived inconsistencies present in liberalism to which Kekes refers so cogently (e.g., the power of evil in the world, the folly of liberals' approach to equality, the presence of individual autonomy as the core of liberalism). Nevertheless, because "hope springs eternal," I have chosen to continue the "cast of my lot" with liberalism as characterized by its presumed credo. I have been reasonably consistent with Professor Spitz's 10 commandments outlined below briefly (from his "A Credo for Liberals" [pp. 213-215] at the end of his insightful book).

1. Esteem liberty above all other values, even over equality and justice.
2. Respect people, not property, but do not ignore the positive role of property in promoting human well-being.
3. Distrust power, even that of majorities.
4. Distrust authority.
5. Be tolerant.
6. Adhere to democracy.
7. Revere truth and rationality.
8. Accept the inevitability of change.
9. Do not disparage compromise.
10. Above all, retain the critical spirit.

Selection 5
Confronting a Conflicting Miasma of Ethical Values

In considering humankind's basic problems, the late Edwin A. Burtt (1965) believed that:

> The greatest danger to his future lies in the
> disturbing emotions and destructive passions that
> he has not yet overcome; the greatest promise lies
> in his capacity for a sensitive understanding of
> himself and his human fellows, and his power to
> enter the inclusive universe in which the creative
> aspirations of all can move freely toward their
> fulfillment (p. 311).

If our "distorting emotions and destructive passions" do indeed represent the greatest danger for the future, the application of a sound approach--whichever one is finally chosen--to personal and professional living can be of inestimable assistance to people who are truly seeking a "sensitive understanding" of themselves and their fellows.

This need for greater ethical awareness and understanding became especially pertinent to me in the late 1960s. At that point, and then continuing through the intervening decades, there is evidence from a variety of sources that others saw this need for study about ethics as well. For example, *The New York Times* reported a generation ago (1978) that "nowadays students in many disciplines are enrolling in new ethics courses in a variety of undergraduate departments and professional programs . . . part of the impetus for new programs stems from the social consciousness of the 1960s" (Feb. 26). Whether this enrollment in such courses could have been shown to have a direct relationship with the earlier social consciousness felt by some in the late 1960s and early 1970s is an interesting, but debatable question.

Nevertheless, it is true that there were many indications back then that people's interest in ethics was increasing. Some examples of this heightened interest, selected from the 1975-1978 period, are (1) Geoffrey Hazard's (1978) article on "Capitalist Ethics"; (2) Henry Fairlie's (1978) book titled The Seven Deadly Sins Today; (3) James Chace's (1977) piece inquiring "How 'moral' can we get?"; (4) Michael Blumenthal's (1977) statement that societal changes have occasioned "questionable and illegal corporate activities"; (5) *The New York Times*' (1976) article asking whether the growing dishonesty in sports was just a reflection of the American society; Derek Bok's (1976) request, as president of Harvard University, that courses in applied ethics be taught; and (7) Amitai Etzioni's (1976) assertion that the "hottest new item" in the Post-Watergate curriculum was "moral education".

And, if the above indications from the 1975-1978 period aren't sufficient to indicate the heightening interest in ethics, there were also (8) Gene Maeroff's (1976) review stressing that "West Point cheaters have a lot of company"; (9) Russell Baker's (1976) spoof implying that good "sports went out with bamboo vaulting poles; (10) Rainer Martens' belief that kid sports may at that time be a "den of iniquity"; (11) Ann Dennis' (1975) article explaining that the Canadian Sociology and Anthropology Association was considering the adoption of a code of ethics; (12) *The Saturday Review* (1975) special report titled "Watergating on Main Street" that assessed the ethics of congressmen, lawyers, businessmen, accountants, journalists, physicians, and educators; and (13) Fred Hechinger's (1974) query as to "Whatever became of sin?" As well, the reader should keep in mind that these references are just an unreliable sampling of the many articles and other statements that surfaced during that period of approximately three years.

Ethics Yesterday and Today

Actually a number of scholarly philosophic texts do treat ethics and morality in great detail. However, they would not serve the purpose I have in mind here. I want to help popularize a subject that should now, as well as in the past, attract much greater attention in the area of general education within the public schools and college.

The first point to be made here is that, in ethics typically, the terms "right" and "wrong" apply only to the acts of a person, whereas "good" and "bad" refer to (1) the effects of acts; (2) the motives from which the act was done; (3) the intention of the person carrying out the deed; and (4) the person who is the agent of a particular act. So, to offer an example, we might say correctly that "although Mike Smith is a good person, he acted wrongly--with good motives and intentions--when he struck Tom Jones and broke his nose. The consequences of Smith's act were bad, even though Jones had made threatening gestures at Smith's smaller brother."

Interestingly, but confusingly, as is the case with so many words and terms that we use nowadays, the term "ethics"* is employed typically in three ways. Each of these has a relation to the other, and all three ways will be used here. First, the term "ethics" is used to classify a general pattern or "way of life" (e.g., normative Christian or Jewish ethics). Second, it refers to a listing of rules of conduct, or what is also called a moral code (e.g., the ethics of a priest, a teacher, or a physician). Thirdly, it has come to be used when describing inquiry about ways of life or rules of conduct (e.g., that subdivision of philosophy now known as meta-ethics).

History substantiates that ethics is a description of "irregular progress toward complete clarification of each type of ethical judgment" (*Encyclopedia of Philosophy*, III, 1967, p. 82). If this is so, how does one judge exactly, or even generally, how much "irregular progress" has been made since the early development of ancient Greek ethics with--say--Socrates in the fifth century B.C.E.? One could argue, for example, that the changing political, economic, and other social forces of that time required the introduction of a new way of conduct. Yet, one could also state that today starting the 21st century there appears to be an urgent need for altered standards of conduct during what is often called a transitional period.

It would be an obvious exaggeration today to say that there are as many views of ethics and/or moral philosophy as there are philosophers. Conversely, however, there is still no single, non-controversial, foundation stone upon which to build the entire structure of ethics. This is not to say that there are not some aspects of this branch of philosophy upon which there have been fairly wide agreement. For example, Noel-Smith (1954) explained in mid-century that moral philosophers in the past offered general guidance as to what to do, what to seek, and how to treat others--injunctions that all of us could well keep in mind still today.

As a rule, philosophers have not preached to their adherents in the same way that theologians of most religions have felt constrained to do. However, down through the centuries many did offer practical advice that included pronouncements on what was good or bad, or right and wrong. Further, many have searched persistently for a true moral code, a normative ethical system upon which people could and should base their conduct. With the advent in the Western world of what has been called philosophical analysis in an "Age of Analysis"--in the Western, English-speaking world at least--as a distinct emphasis or approach to this day, the contemporary analytic philosopher was thrust into the middle of the struggle between the ethical objectivist and the ethical subjectivist. (The ethical objectivist had been working toward the creation of a true moral code, whereas the subjectivist argued conversely that such objectivity was not reasonable--or even possible. As the subjectivist saw it, the achievement of objectivity in a true moral code was definitely not possible. Thus, it simply not possible to state that any such knowledge could prescribe how people should live.)

As a result of such indecision and controversy, and at the very time when the world society appears to be in the throes of a momentous transition, the large majority of philosophical scholars are almost completely silent on the subject of morality and ethics. Further in a period when the world's turmoil is also characterized by "hot" wars, "cold" wars, expanding treaty organizations, terrorists, or what have you, in place of offering a "guide to the perplexed" (with thanks to Maimonides, the great Jewish philosopher and physician of the Middle Ages), the practitioners in this same profession of philosophy avoid the rational justification of any type of moral system for public consumption. Admittedly there has been some movement in the direction of rectifying this imbalance, but the bulk of these scholars continue to analyze the meaning and function of moral concepts and statements in a more or less scientific and/or logical manner. In the process the average intelligent adult with a college degree, much less a high-school degree, is receiving no help in coping with life's great questions from the field of philosophy.

While this analytic approach was growing and strengthening typically in the eyes of most members of departments of philosophy in North America, others in diverse fields have been filling the gap created by offering prescriptive and normative advice freely down through the years of the twentieth century to the present. Accordingly, also, because some of us were evidently afraid to be challenged as illogical, hortatory, careless thinkers by our own colleagues within philosophy and its departmental philosophies, the field of ethics and morality as applied to life generally--in politics, in business and economics, in science, in medicine, in education, and even in sport and fitness--was left to people who usually have given the topic much less careful thought than we as individuals within the field have/

Here I am referring, of course, to dramatists, theologians, novelists, poets, physicians, politicians, educational administrators, business leaders--in no special order of importance--who offer a great variety of opinions, ranging from suggestions to recommendations, to prescriptions, and to dogma, about what is good and bad, right and wrong, about all aspects of life. Most notable among these categories of "philosophers" recently are scientists, politicians, and comedians, people who may have earned justifiable fame--or even notoriety.

The Present Situation in Philosophy Is Intolerable

This point should not be carried too far. So, I will simply state that this present situation, one in which there has developed such a sharp distinction between the relatively few moral philosophers concerned with normative ethics and the much larger number involved with some form of critical or analytic philosophy, should in my opinion be rectified as soon as possible The matter of values that ultimately govern our social system and culture is far too vital to leave almost completely to those who can be classified as laymen with no training or professionals from other fields with quite possibly a built-in bias. What I would hope is that a steadily increasing number of trained philosophers would spend more time on providing helpful advice to the public and accordingly less time on what often seems to be "scientific pedantry."

I am pleased to be able state parenthetically that there are others who tend to agree with this opinion. These are qualified philosophers who felt that the pendulum had swung too far in one direction in the "Age of Analysis." One example of such a belief was the late Richard Rorty's 1982 essay titled "Philosophy in America today" in which he decried those who concentrate only on philosophical problem-solving in a "scientific" manner. He explained: "The situation in moral and social philosophy, admittedly, is not the same as in the so-called 'central' areas of philosophy. Here we have Rawls' Theory of justice as a genuine inter-university paradigm, a book whose importance and permanence are deservedly recognized on all sides" (p. 216).

Another example, speaking in a similar vein as Rorty about the same time, was John E. Smith (1982). In his presidential address to the American Philosophical Association, also complained that "the decline of philosophy as an influential voice in the intellectual exchange within our culture has been the result of several questionable conceptions that have dominated much of modern philosophy since the seventeenth century" (p. 7). Before offering specific conditions that he believed might contribute to the "recovery of philosophy as a significant force in American society" (p. 10), Smith also bemoaned the fact that so many questions of importance to humanity had been abandoned by the bulk of scholars "doing" philosophy (p. 8).

Further, many of us who are specializing in what have been called "departmental" philosophies need scholarly guidance in the subject of ethics as applied to our professions. Here I am referring to such specialties as medical ethics, business ethics, legal ethics, sport ethics, educational ethics, or what have you. We need to understand more fully what the relationship could be, or even should be, between normative ethics and meta-ethics. There are extremists, of course, but a more reasonable approach to follow would seem to be one in which a moral philosopher or ethical theorist-- whether he or she is employed in the mother discipline or in, say, a department of educational philosophy (such as existed formerly)--can engage in metaethical analysis if desired, or can become involved in a scholarly approach to normative analysis without fear of unreasonable reprisal in one way or another by colleagues of an opposite persuasion.

Rorty (1982) would support this position, since he explicitly stated that philosophers of the analytic persuasion "should relax and say, with our colleagues in history and literature, that we in the humanities differ from our natural scientists precisely in not knowing in advance what our problems are, and in not needing to provide criteria of identity. . . ." (p. 218). In other words, all should be working toward the elimination of irrational ethical beliefs while attempting to discover the soundest possible approach to ethical decision-making for our evolving society.

Normative Ethical Inquiry

As we move ahead in our consideration of ethical decision-making, I should make clear that the task of normative ethical inquiry can also be difficult, especially when complex issues and specific conclusions tend to stray into the realm of meta-ethics as well. (Meta-ethics may be defined as inquiry as to the nature of human morality and conduct with regard to the definition, purposes, presuppositions, methodology, and limitations of the subject. Of course, it is not the purpose of this book to follow this approach solely, or even largely.)

For example, it is quite simple to distinguish between a normative ethical statement such as "Harsh teaching methods have no place in education" and a meta-ethical statement such as "A teacher knows through intuition whether his/her beliefs about teaching ethics are fundamentally true." Further, when a normative ethical theory such as hedonism--i.e., an ethical doctrine that states humans should guide their conduct on the basis of personal pleasure (however defined) such conduct will bring--such as "Religious teaching is good because it brings pleasure," the non-hedonist could well challenge this statement solely on the meaning of the terms "good" and "pleasure." Obviously, the difficulty of justifying a normative ethical theory brings to the fore penetrating questions about meta-ethical relativism and subjectivism. And when such questions as these are carefully pursued, they point up the present severity of the "subjectivist threat" to what may be called "normative objectivism."

Basically and fundamentally, then, justification of an ethical theory, or even an incomplete set of ethical statements about education, religion, sport, or any other aspect of life revolves around the ability of the theorist to (1) state correctly, (2) elucidate sufficiently, and (3) defend adequately his or her moral or ethical values and claims. This means answering a variety of questions. For example, is a moral judgment objective or subjective? Does a moral judgment differ from a factual judgment? Is an ethical statement about right conduct in medicine, law, or education publicly warrantable? (In other words, is there some publicly acceptable procedure for verification that reasonable people would be willing to accept?) Finally, should ethical claims be objectively verifiable, and should they be universalizable? (If so, this would make such claims practical for use in everyday life.)

Definitions and Clarification

Moving ahead to further basic information about ethics and morality, there are several further points that require definition and clarification. For example, we should keep in mind the distinction between statements of fact as opposed to statements of value. In the first instance, I might argue that "health is desired" (a fact in this instance), whereas I might also state that "health is desirable" for everyone (actually a statement of value on my part).

We should keep in mind, also, that there are two fields of value theory in philosophy--ethics and aesthetics. As explained earlier, in ethics we are involved with matters of good and bad, right and wrong, duty and obligation, and moral responsibility. In aesthetics, however, value is viewed somewhat differently. In this case we take into consideration matters or doctrines of taste or beauty, meaning, and truth--all typically considered within an art context.

From another standpoint, we need to keep in mind that, although the word "good" is central to the subject of ethics, most of the times we use it we are actually not expressing moral judgments (e.g., "good apple," "good road," "good game of tennis"). Thus, if we say, "this is a good X," usually we mean that X fulfills, to a higher or greater degree than most X's, the criterion (or criteria) for which this particular X is designed or intended.

However, it is when we use the word "good" in moral discussions that a variety of problems arise. For example, we might state that Jones exhibits "good" character when he plays tennis, or that Jones shows "good" intentions when he helped Thompson up after accidentally driving the tennis ball into his face. Further, Jones might also have made "good" moves when he later played a doubles match in tennis. And so it goes. . . . Nevertheless, the main moral words used in ethics are "good," "bad," "right," and "wrong," but confusion often develops when we use one or more of them in specific contexts.

Still further, we need to keep in mind that ethics today is typically divided into two main categories, only the first of which will be discussed here: (1) normative ethics is an attempt to discover a rational and possibly acceptable view that may be defended concerning those things that are good in this world (i.e., worth aiming at or working for) and what kinds of acts are right (and why this is so); and (2) metaethics is a field of inquiry that considers the meaning of words regarded as ethical and moral, as well as the actual inter-relations of such meanings. In this latter area, there appear now to be three distinct metaethical theories that have gradually emerged:

a. Ethical naturalism, a position in which it is argued that ethical sentences can be translated into non-ethical ones without losing their meaning (usually a difficult accomplishment),

b. Ethical non-naturalism, a position in which it is argued that at least some ethical sentences cannot be translated into any other kinds of sentences (this constitutes an autonomous class), and

c. Ethical non-cognitivism, a position in which it is argued that ethical sentences do not express any propositions at all.

The Ethical Problem in Life

With this introductory material behind us, we are in a better position to consider the essence of "the ethical problem" as it appears in life. My personal belief is that an ethical problem cannot be correctly delineated unless there is also prior analysis and basic understanding of the values and norms of the prevailing social system and culture in which a person lives.

What is most important for our understanding at this point is that the various subsystems of society together compose a hierarchy of control and conditioning. For example, in Parsonsian "action theory," these subsystems total four: (1) culture, (2) social system, (3) personality, and (4) behavioral organism. Moreover, just as there are four subsystems within the total action system (as defined by Parsons and others), there appear to be, also, four levels within the particular subsystem known as "social system" (indicated as the second level immediately above).

These levels, proceeding from "highest" to "lowest," are (2a) values, (2b) norms, (2c) the structure of collectivities, and (2d) the structure of roles. Typically, the higher levels are more general than the lower ones, with the latter giving specific guidance to those segments or units of the particular system to which they apply. These "units" or "segments" are either collectivities or individual in their capacity as role occupants.

This delineation no doubt seems to be complex, and it is; however, the important thing to keep in mind is that the hierarchy of control and conditioning operates or functions in both downward and upward directions! Typically, the greatest pressure for conformity is exerted downward by the values and norms operative within a social system at a given time. In the United States the most important social values are (1) the rule of law, (2) the socio-structural facilitation of individual achievement, and (3) the equality of opportunity.

Similar to values, but which should be distinguished from them, are the norms of the social system. Norms are the shared, sanctioned rules that govern the second level of the social structure. People often find it difficult to understand the differentiation between the concepts of "value" and "norm."

Keeping the above listing of values in mind, compare and contrast them with the following examples of norms in the United States; (1) the institution of private property; (2) private enterprise; (3) the monogamous, conjugal family; and (4) the separation of church and state (Johnson, 1969, pp. 46-47).

Keeping the above discussion in mind, and understanding that there are a number of cultures and social systems in the world, you can now comprehend how a great many problems involving the stability of values and norms can spring up just about any day at any time in any place. For example, consider the gradual shattering of the amateur ideal that has occurred in Olympic sport, an ideal propounded before the revival of the Olympic Games in 1896. Or, as another example, think how we witnessed displays of unbridled nationalism when top North American professional hockey players had their titanic struggles with Russian "amateurs" for supremacy in a sport that since then has become increasingly marred by undue violence at every turn.

Of course, sharp diversity of opinion and belief can exist--publicly, that is--only in a social system within a culture characterized by pluralistic (i.e., a number of) philosophies both within the philosophical mainstream or in the various departmental philosophies of the mother discipline (e.g., educational philosophy). Such a condition is not necessarily bad, of course. It undoubtedly requires a political state in which a considerable amount of participatory democracy is present. Interestingly, the paradoxical opinion is often expressed that North America functions in a materialistic fashion despite being described typically as possessing an overarching, almost inherent philosophic idealism.

Many people today are absolutely convinced that all of the old standards and morals have been completely negated. As a result they believe that the world is "going to Hell in the proverbial hand basket." Accordingly, they argue, only a return to earlier (presumably!) halcyon days can prevent impending disaster. So they decry what they believe are evident "situation" ethics,* because they sense an uncharted course ahead on a rocky road leading to perdition (i.e., total disaster).

Oddly enough, as described above briefly, at the very time when people seem to need guidance, many have turned away from organized religion. Also, a very large percentage of philosophers, in the English-speaking world at least, seemed to have quite completely abandoned a function accepted formerly for their field for today's strictly disciplinary (analytic/meta-ethical) approach to their work. Of course, this latter development (i.e., a strictly disciplinary approach to their task) was actually a direction followed by many other disciplines to a great extent since mid-century. In the 1960s, for example, a similar disciplinary orientation occurred in educational philosophy and then, during the 1970s, this trend spread to sport and physical activity philosophy as well.

As I see it, the swing of the pendulum was too great (it was ever thus!). And, to confuse the issue even further, the general public has incorporated such words as pragmatism*, idealism*, realism*, and existentialism* into their vocabulary. As a result the original meaning of these philosophic terms or stances have been (possibly) forever distorted beyond recognition. The result is that current use of these terms today now requires extensive qualification.

All of the above adds up to the conclusion that society has now moved to the point where unanimity is often lacking in regard to "what's good," "what's bad," or whether such distinction makes all that much difference any more. This conclusion is obviously extreme, of course, but it is true that the distinction between the everyday concepts (or meanings) of "good" and "bad" has indeed become blurred at present--no matter what phase of life is under consideration.

I well recall this point being brought home forcibly over a generation ago by Cogley (1972) when he wrote:

> Every major institution in the land and most of the minor ones as well seemed to have been caught up in an identity crisis. Upheavals in the church were front-page news for almost a decade. The revolt again the prevailing idea of a university which began in Berkeley in 1964 kept erupting with dismaying frequency. Veteran army officers found themselves at a loss as to how to deal with rebellious troops. The Democratic debacle at the Chicago convention four years ago dramatized a widespread disillusionment with the political parties. . . .

And, if all of this wasn't bad enough, he continued as follows:

> The once sacrosanct public school system came under severe attack. Working newsmen who took to producing their own underground newspapers after hours voiced bitter disenchantment with the established press employing them. So prevalent was the discontent within the academic and professional communities that the "radical caucuses" within them were given semi-official status. Bishops, university presidents, military brass, publishers, politicians, school principals, and other established "leaders," it became increasingly clear, were no longer leading...(p. 2).

In retrospect we now appreciate that the values, norms, and standards of morality of the 1960s did indeed undergo an identity crisis that has endured to a considerable extent since that time. To be sure, there has been the usual swinging of the pendulum in the other direction since. Yet many of the same problems, often in slightly "different clothes," have emerged again in the late 1990s and early years of the present century. No one can deny that the subject of personal and professional ethics is today still in a state of flux and will warrant careful monitoring on into the indeterminate future.

Concluding Statement

It is indeed true that the world seems to be more "rudderless" than previously, and who can argue against this position successfully? The implications for us all personally and professionally is that we need to develop a greatly improved understanding of, and approach to, possible solutions for these ongoing, ever-changing moral and ethical problems and issues. The "waves will flow to and fro" indefinitely for better or worse. It seems obvious that all of us need to become more seriously involved in this matter of ethical decision-making.

References

Baker, R. (1976). Good bad sports. *The New York Times Magazine*, Feb. 1.

Blumenthal, W. M. (1977). Business morality has not deteriorated--society has changed. *The New York Times*, Jan. 9.

Bok, D. C. (1975). Can ethics be taught? *Change*, 8, 9:26-30.

Burtt, E. A. (1965). *In search of philosophical understanding*. NY: New American Library.

Chace, J. (1977). How "moral" can we get? *The New York Times Magazine*, May 22.

Cogley, J. (July/August, 1972). The storm before the calm. *The Center Magazine* V (4), 2-3.

Coles, R. (1997). *The moral intelligence of children*. NY: Random House.

Dennis, Ann B. (1975). A code of ethics for sociologists and anthropologists? *Social Sciences in Canada*, 3 (1-2):14-16.

Encyclopedia of Philosophy, The (8 vols.) (P. Edwards, Ed.). (1967). NY: Macmillan and The Free Press.

Etzioni, A. (1976). Do as I say, not as I do. *The New York Times Magazine*, Sept. 26.

Fairlie, H. (1978). *The seven deadly sins today*. Washington, DC: New Republic.

Goldman, D. (1995). *Emotional intelligence*. NY: Bantam.

Hazard, G. C., Jr. (1978). Capitalist ethics. *Yale Alumni Magazine & Journal*, XLI, 8:50-51.

Hechinger, F. M. (1974). Whatever became of sin? *Saturday Review/World*, Sept. 24.

Johnson, H. M. (1969). The relevance of the theory of action to historians. *Social Science Quarterly*, 2:46-68.

Maeroff, G. I. (1976). West Point cheaters have a lot of company. *The New York Times*, June 20.

Martens, R. (1976). Kid sports: A den of iniquity or land of promise? *Proceedings of the 79th Annual Meeting, NCPEAM* (Gedvilas, L. L., Ed.). Chicago, IL: Univ. of Illinois, Chicago.

New York Times, The. (1976). The growing dishonesty in

sports: Is it just a reflection of our American society?
Nov. 7.

New York Times, The (1978). The ethical imperative, Feb.
26.

Nowell-Smith, P. H. (1954). *Ethics.* Harmondsworth, England.

Rorty, R. (1982) Philosophy in America today. In
Consequences of Pragmatism (Essays: 1972-1980) (pp.
211-230. Minneapolis, MN: Univ. of Minnesota Press.

Smith, J. E. (1982) The need for a recovery of philosophy.
*Proceedings of the Seventy-Eighth Meeting of the
American Philosophical Association,* 56, 5-18.

Wright, R. (1994). *The moral animal.* NY: Pantheon.

Selection 6
Orientating Philosophically to Pragmatism

Generally speaking, I inevitably found myself agreeing with the philosophical position that ended up with the name "pragmatism." Adherents to this atypical stance proceed on the assumption that it is only possible to find out if something is worthwhile only through experience. This approach is not new in the Earth's history, of course, but 19th- and 20th-century pragmatism organized this type of thinking into a philosophic stance now accepted in many quarters, especially in scientific and educational circles.

There are some who believe that pragmatism's theory about the acquisition of knowledge (epistemology) looms so large in the consideration of this position that this aspect of the philosophy must be discussed first. This may be true from one standpoint, but I will persist here with the traditional sequential categorical pattern recognized in the discipline of philosophy.

Metaphysics

It has often been said that this philosophical position has no interest in a general worldview and that method is its only concern. This statement may be partially true; yet, the assertion that the pragmatist is so extremely narrow in this regard must be rejected. It is doubtful whether any rational being ever goes through life without many, many times asking questions as to the basic "whys and wherefores" of the universe in which he or she lives.

The pragmatist has arrived at the stage where she realizes that it is beyond the human's power to do anything about the course of the physical universe. She believes further that a person is only deluding herself when she attempts to speculate about the infinite. Her problem, therefore, is to interpret what she finds. She looks at nature and, quite naturally, she asks questions about it: (1) How is it to be interpreted? (2) Is nature an inexorable process that is advancing according to a universal plan? (3) Is the onward surge of nature a kind of emergent evolution? To the question of interpretation of nature, the pragmatist says that she will take what she finds and function from there. To the question as to whether Nature is an inexorable process working according to a universal plan, she maintains that she doesn't actually know. At times she probably hopes so, because this would certainly afford a sense of security; but, for the greater part of the time she hopes not--individual freedom as possible is much too important a matter for her.

The pragmatist believes that scientific fact has proved that nature is indeed an emergent evolution; yet, this raises a further question in her mind--emerging toward what? This philosophic position limits our frame of reality to nature as it functions. If a person does make any assumptions about the nature of reality, they are only hypotheses to be held tentatively. The future is always to be considered, because situations are constantly changing. The belief is that the ongoing process cannot be dealt with finally at any one time. Activity must be related to past experience as well.

The World Is Characterized by Activity and Change. Even these preceding statements cannot be considered entirely free from inferences regarding the nature of reality. It is argued that the world is characterized by activity and change. All that is known concerning the human response to nature can be known without first definitely making a final statement about the universe as a whole. Thus, experience or interaction with the environment is all that the pragmatist has by which to lead her life. If her environment doesn't give her an accurate account of reality, then it would seem that humans are the victims of a fantastic hoax (by whomever or whatever invoked it).

The World Is Still Incomplete. The pragmatist believes further in organic evolution and that rational humans have developed in this process. The logical conclusion to draw from this assumption is that the world is still incomplete. This doesn't mean, of course, that everything is in a state of change, nor does it imply that it will ever be complete. Some elements and structures appear to be relatively stable. But this quality of stability is often deceiving; the pragmatist, consequently, looks upon the world as a mixture of things relatively stable and still incomplete. This makes all life a great experiment. At this point it is evidently the task of humans and their educational system to make this experiment as intelligent a one as possible.

Theory of Emergent Novelty. If reality is indeed constantly undergoing change, how, asks the pragmatist, could education remain essentially the same from one generation to the next? From the evidence on hand, the pragmatist will certainly not accept the idea that there is an end to progress. Progressive education as defined by the pragmatist, for example, is a process of continuous growth to meet the needs and interests of a changing person in a changing society in a changing world. Brubacher (1939, p. 35), in all four editions of his major philosophical text, offered an example of novelty that struck a strong blow against the opposing theorists who maintained that any emergence is merely the uncovering of some antecedent reality. He explained that each and every baby born "is inescapably unique since any given offspring of bisexual reproduction is the only one of its kind. Such a child commences and lives his life at a juncture of space and time which simply cannot be duplicated for anyone else." If this is indeed novelty, according to its definition, then the future must, of necessity, be uncertain in outcome. Thus, the physical and social environment of the pragmatist is characterized by the constant possibility of novelty, precariousness, and unpredictability, since life and education are the interaction of humans and their environment.

The Idea of Freedom of Will. Many of the philosophical positions include statements about freedom of will. However, this is definitely one of the strong points of pragmatism over against the more traditional positions. The human's future must allow for freedom of will. Free will is not conceived of as a motiveless choice, and the pragmatist's position on this point certainly clashes with the essentialist (i.e., the idealist or realist) who allows for enough free will so the world can unfold properly. The pragmatist's contention is that all beings are in interaction with other "existences." She inquires about the quality of this interaction and asks further how great a role the individual can play in this process. She would urge investigation to determine the character of this process from within. As the pragmatist understands life, the individual truly learns from experience. Thus, for each individual, the inclination to learn from activity and experience will be accepted gradually and subsequently as fully developed as possible. Freedom developed in this manner is achieved through continuous and developmental learning from experience. J. L. Childs (1931, p. 168), the strongly progressive philosopher of education, explained the problem of freedom and education in one of his early works as follows: "In a changing world the only person who can become free and who can maintain his freedom is the one who has 'learned to learn.' A democratic society can hope to succeed only if it is composed of individuals who have developed the responsibility for intelligent self-direction in cooperation with others." Obviously, if we learn what we practice, then schooling must be placed on an experience basis. Only in this way will people increase their ability to control their own experience--which is freedom!

Epistemology

Earlier in this section, I explained that some felt this aspect of pragmatism should be introduced before the others (e.g., before axiology). *The rationale for this belief was that pragmatism starts with a theory of knowledge-acquisition, not a metaphysical statement of belief.* A serious difficulty arises here immediately. Why? It does simply because an adequate definition of knowledge has tried the insight and ingenuity of learned men and women for many centuries right down to the present day. If knowledge is fact, and fact is truth, then truth is knowledge. Knowledge has been described as a *knowing-about-something, an awareness, a comprehension, or an understanding.* Here it becomes a subjective matter, and it has to do with the inner workings of the mind. Still others believe in a type of knowledge called *objective*--knowledge existing in the world outside the conscious, perceiving individual. Such knowledge is there to be known, grasped, and mastered by an intellect (a human one only?). Up to this point, knowledge may be defined as something that is known or can be known. However, the difficulty does not end at this point. There are other problems about knowledge that have troubled many as follows:

(1) What does it consist of?
(2) How does the person truly know what she believes she knows?
(3) Can human knowledge comprehend all?
(4) Is it possible for humans to have knowledge about the infinite?

Questions such as these above could be legion.

Some Historical Background. After hundreds of years of speculation, there gradually arose a body of evidence called the (social) science of psychology. This is a separate branch of study that examines the processes of the mind and the varied states of knowing in the individual mind. Locke said that all knowledge must come through experience--that is, it must be obtained by means of the senses. Kant maintained that there was also knowledge that has not been experienced; in fact, his theory of *der Ding an sich* (the thing-in-itself) asserted that there is a realm of reality that cannot be known by humans. Still later, Hegel considered this issue and argued that "the real" is in the mind--a manifestation of intelligence.

A New Theory of Mind. Modern scientific development, after Darwin's evolutionary theory, opened the way for a new theory of knowledge--the pragmatic idea of knowledge and truth. This seemed to make sense in a world where scientific method was influencing almost all thought, marching on with great rapidity. William James took the lead in espousing this theory in which knowledge is a result of a process of thought with a useful purpose. Truth is not only to be tested by its correspondence with reality, but also by its practical results. This pragmatic treatment of knowledge lies between the extremes of reason and sense perception, with some ideas that are not included in either rationalism or empiricism. Truth, therefore, not only *is* true, but it *becomes* true. Knowledge is not present because it has been acquired through the years; it is there because it has been earned through experience. It must work. It is an instrument of verification. This type of knowledge, which is literally "wrought in action," should help in the battle for human survival.

The Function of Mind. The pragmatist naturalizes mind by making it a normal part of nature. As Brubacher (1962, p. 60) explained, the pragmatist "adopts the evolutionary viewpoint that mind has evolved in the natural order as a more flexible means of adapting the organism to a changing environment." Thus, if the mind were not functioning, the human would lose control of Earth. This is a mind, therefore, that helps humans to form knowledge or truth by undergoing experience. It must be adaptable because of the possibility of novelty and the consequent precariousness of the human's relationship with the world.

The Relation of Body and Mind to the Learning Process. The pragmatic position, in connection with this problem, is more or less of an intermediate one. It does not coincide with the position of the behaviorist, who believes that the mind and the central nervous system are identical--that the mind is therefore only another bodily organ. Conversely, the pragmatist rejects the postulate that the mind is immaterial and entirely extraneous from the body. The experience of the mind must be taken into consideration in order to satisfy the pragmatist. That the mind and the body interact, he does not deny. It is precisely this interaction that concerns him. Mind, through evolution, has become that part of the whole of the human that enables him to cope with the surrounding world. Through experience, the human's many problems have been, are, and will be solved. An intelligent mind makes this possible.

Dewey's Experimental Method. This theory of knowledge led to John Dewey's experimental method for the solving of problems that is characterized by the following steps:

1. Life is characterized by movement, the smoothness of whose flow may be interrupted by an obstacle.
2. This obstacle creates a problem; the resultant tension must be resolved to allow further movement to take place.
3. The human marshals all available and pertinent facts to help with the solution of the problem.
4. The data gathered fall into one or more patterns; subsequent analysis offers a working hypothesis.
5. This hypothesis must be tested to see if the problem may be solved through the application of the particular hypothesis chosen.

When the problem is solved, movement may begin again. A hypothesis that turns out to be true offers a frame of reference for organizing facts; subsequently, this results in a central meaning that may be called knowledge. *The pragmatic theory of knowledge acquisition (epistemology) merges with its value theory at this point,* inasmuch as such knowledge frees the human to initiate subsequent action furthering the process of movement and change.

Logic

There seems to be rather general agreement that logic is primarily concerned with the methods of reasoning that humans employ in their search to find answers for the problems that confront them. From this rather general definition, one could make a good case for the argument that logic is the most fundamental branch of philosophy. Thinking and reasoning are necessary for study of all aspects of this subject. Consequently the importance of correct thinking is self-evident.

A Radical Departure from Traditional Logic. As you might expect, pragmatism is a philosophy that represents a radical departure from traditional logic. Dewey (1938, p. 98), as the recognized leader of this philosophical approach, decried the inadequacy of Aristotelian logic since he felt it to be out of place in the 20th century. He reasoned that a system of logic that regarded nature as a fixed system simply could not meet the challenge of a universe that seemed to be boundless and perhaps expanding. What Dewey desired was a revised system of logic--"a unified theory of inquiry through which the authentic pattern of experimental and operational inquiry in science shall become available for regulation of the habitual methods by which inquiries in the field of common sense are carried on."

The Pattern of Logic. How shall we interpret this seemingly difficult statement by Dewey? Obviously, the pattern of logic recommended bears a strong relationship to the learning theory described above under the epistemology of pragmatism. Dewey speaks first of *the indeterminate situation* which raises doubt in an individual's mind. The second stage is called *institution of a problem* and takes place when a person realizes the indeterminacy of the situation and the need for clarification of the issue or problem. Next in order is the *determination of a problem-solution*, which is basically the same as the establishment of a hypothesis in a scientific experiment. At this point we find the introduction of ideas that may be instrumental in determining the solution to the problem-situation. The fourth stage as outlined by Dewey is called *reasoning*. Possible solutions may come to mind as answers, but they never seem to fit the problem-situation in exactly the same way as they may have done previously. Hence an adaptation with possible subsequent modifications takes place that must be reasoned through with extreme care. It is important to understand that Dewey treats facts as functional inasmuch as they contribute to the movement toward solution of the problem. This is referred to as *the operational character of the facts-meaning.* It is difficult for us to comprehend how meanings are closely related to operations, mainly because they are, in a sense, inseparable from it as they give direction to any further observation as the problem-solution movement takes place.

This pattern of logic is fascinating largely because it appears to bridge the gap between traditional logic and what we know as "scientific inquiry". Butler (1957, p. 464), for example, emphasized how the pattern of logic available to science can be employed by the average person in daily, common-sense, problem-situations. It creates a two-way street, because scientific inquiry now has a common-sense base.

Butler pointed out further four *characterizations of the pattern* that make it such an innovation (pp. 264-266). First, patterns of thought peculiar to induction and deduction cannot be applied to a problem-situation arbitrarily, since each situation is unique. Second, there is a very close relationship between this pattern of logic and life as we know it--in other words, the human and Nature are continuous. Third, such a pattern of logic seems to fit human sociological development as well as human biological progress. Last, it is interesting to note that such an approach to logic has applications for individual as well as group and societal problems.

> Note: Because of the importance of this topic and the development of interest in *critical thinking* (or informal logic), this approach is described substantively in E. F. Zeigler's *Critical Thinking for the Professions: Health, Sport & Physical Education, Recreation, and Dance.* Champaign, IL: Stipes Publishing L.L.C., 1994. A second reason for mentioning it here is that pragmatism's approach to logic, as explained above, is distinctly different from that of idealism and realism. However, this fact does not invalidate the use of critical thinking (or informal logic).

Axiology

The system of values of the philosophy of pragmatism is necessarily consistent with the other aspects of this philosophical tendency. *A value is that fact which, when applied to life, becomes useful.* An experience is adjudged as valuable by the human organism which is attempting to adapt itself to the environment in the best and most profitable manner. The comparison of values in order to determine the best ones is a problem of deciding which value or values will help achieve life's purposes in the best way. Yet it is important to understand that these goals may only be temporary.

What are the main values? For the pragmatist that depends on the when, where, and how the individual is living. Innumerable attempts have been made to set various standards and value systems for people living in modern, complex society. The pragmatist, according to Geiger (1955, p. 142), believes that "values must be closely related to the world in which man finds himself." The human simply should choose which means and ends he or she will accept and which will be rejected. Progress depends upon critical examination of values before intelligent selection.

Ethically, the pragmatist is continually facing new situations in which wise judgment must be exercised in keeping with the apparent elements of the indeterminate situation. Pragmatism offers the possibility of resolving what has been most troublesome in ethical behavior up to this time–how to resolve a situation where one's motives are good, but the individual's action violates currently acceptable standards. When the pragmatic steps of logic are employed, progressing from:

(1) the indeterminate situation through
(2) the institution of a problem,
(3) to the determination of a problem-solution,
(4) to reasoning, and
(5) to the operational character of facts-meaning for further observation of the proposed course of action, it is possible to blend inner motives and outer behavior in planned, purposeful action to meet each new situation in a fresh, unbiased manner.

Aesthetically, we are concerned with experiences that convey beauty and meaning of an enduring nature. For the pragmatist, aesthetic appreciation is closely related to the nature of the experience. In life we fluctuate between tension and pleasure depending on whether indeterminate situations are resolved to our satisfaction. When we find the answers to our problems, tensions are eased and enjoyment results. It is noted, however, that there is no permanent state of aesthetic pleasure for a human, since life's rhythm of experience does not function in such a way as to make this possible. Thus, aesthetic satisfaction comes when close identification is maintained with the ebb and flow of life's indeterminate situations. We are all anxious to preserve a state of enjoyment and release.

However, if such a "state" is held too long and disturbs life's rhythm, troublesome difficulties arise. The psychological problems arising from life in a dream world are only too well known. Fortunately, various categories of artists help us to freeze many of these aesthetic values for subsequent enjoyment. The person who would achieve the greatest amount of aesthetic enjoyment must possess and continually develop those habits that promote keen insight. Finally, it should be mentioned that Dewey assigned a lesser role to values that are the opposite of beauty. For example, tragedy and horror may be preserved as art forms. As we look back at these past experiences of our own, or of others, we can feel this experience in some perspective and accept it with calm mien as a form of beauty.

Religiously, the pragmatist assumes a completely naturalistic approach. Thus, it can be seen that religion would have to be defined in a considerably less orthodox fashion. Any worship of the supernatural is obviously not present. The religious pragmatist would be a person who is most anxious to reach pragmatic values whenever and wherever possible by living purposefully. The human's task is to thrust himself or herself into life's many experiences; only there in life will the pragmatist find the opportunity to give it true meaning.

Socially, we find that the pragmatist places great emphasis on this aspect of life. The achievement of social values is fundamental (*don't mistake this for mere socializing at casual social functions*), since life (or society) is "an organic process upon which individuals depend and by which they live" (Butler, 1957, p. 475). Any individual who would withdraw from regular, significant relationship with others in order to work only for other than social values in life makes a drastic error. Recluses generally injure society by withdrawing from their responsibility to it, and it is quite possible that they do themselves still greater harm. Such social values are loyalty, cooperation, kindness, and generosity can hardly be achieved in a vacuum. The pragmatist sees the highest possible relationship between the individual and the society existing in a democracy. Pragmatic values are most in evidence when the individual has the opportunity to develop to the highest of his or her potentialities--so long as this development does not interfere with the good of the whole. It is impossible to develop many of the social values described above to the same extent in certain other types of society. The pragmatist finds a much better balance in a political state characterized by democracy.

Summary.

It can be stated that there are still proponents of idealism, realism, and pragmatism (notably the latter in philosophic circles), and especially in departmental philosophies (e.g., philosophy of education)--not to mention those who believe that the worsening world condition demands an existential-phenomenological orientation. The pendulum swings to and fro, and never seems to stop permanently at any one spot in its arc.

Selection 7
Developing a Pragmatic Approach to Education

Society, School, and the Individual

There is no doubt that pragmatism (sometimes called pragmatic naturalism) has exercised a significant influence on education in he United States as well as in a number of other countries (e.g., Japan). A careful examination would indicate, however, that it has not had as much influence direct influence on program as many of its opponents would have us think it has.

As the pragmatic naturalist sees it, education is very definitely a *social* institution. As a social phenomenon it is actually one of the basic means by which society progresses and regenerates itself/Furthermore, under this philosophic stance, it is a moral affair, a value enterprise. To carry out its true role best, there is no escaping the fact that the school *of necessity* must maintain a close connection with society.

The Individual in a Democratic Society

To understand such a connection, I found it essential to consider the relative importance, educationally speaking, of both the individual and the society. We must resolve the question as to whether the student's development is actually *the* end of education, or whether the interests of the individual should be subordinated to those of the state. In this respect pragmatism and democracy do seem to go hand in hand. As far back as 1934, Burton offered his opinion as to the fundamentals of this democratic philosophy as follows:

> . . . democracy is not equalitarianism, nor majority rule, nor blind conformity, nor ruthless individualism, nor paternalistic guarantee of individual happiness. What, then, is it? It means not only government of, for, and by the people, but also industry, art, science, opportunities for enjoyment, all the activities of the common life to be of, for, and by the common people. Democracy is participatory group life, enjoyed by free individuals possessing maximum opportunities for participation. Its chief characteristic in regard to individuals is, in current happy phase, "respect for

personality." In regard to the group its chief characteristic is the flexible and evolutionary nature of group institutions, free participation in cooperative group life under evolutionary institutions and with respect between individuals are the earmarks of democracy. Democracy is a system of attitudes, social insights, values, and personal disciplines by means of which all men seek and enjoy the good life.

There are noble words, whose proposed goal is even today far from realization. Nevertheless, the plan is that in a democracy there is ample room for individual freedom and development. On the other hand, we can't forget for a minute that sharing is the other great principle of the democratic philosophy of life. The pragmatist believes that, despite certain evident failings of a practical nature that have surfaced, experience is gradually showing that this type of society offers the best solution yet discovered on Earth.

As we can appreciate, of course, in any society the influence of the economic and the political system on education is very great indeed—more in some than in others, of course. If the people of a society have to work from sunup to sundown to maintain a meager existence. Naturally they will not have much of any formal education. Likewise, if a society is run by a group of people who have come into power by force or deception, it is quite possible that the underlings will have little or no opportunity for formalized education. The pragmatist is therefore vitally concerned about a societal medium where he democratic philosophy of life prevails.

The Dual Role of Formalized Education

For the pragmatic naturalist, formalized education serves a dual purpose. The social heritage must be preserved and handed down from generation to generation. The second role is equally as important as the first: it must siphon out the more important qualities of this "intellectual sea" while directing and guiding the student in the formation of new idea s regarding the world. This creative function should in time cause major changes in the structure of the society itself. Each faction, the traditional and the progressive, tends to have a restraining influence on the other. This influence is beneficial in the long run, as it seems to hold radical, possibly harmful, influences in check. If teachers are allowed to present all sides of an issue   at hand and to help the students form independent personal conclusions, they do indeed have the opportunity to become some of the most important leaders in a society.

Which Agency Shall Educate?

Discussion often arises as to which agency shall educate the individual–the home, the school, the state, or some private agency. In resolving this question the most important problem is to determine whether any agency is capable of performing the whole task alone. In a democracy each agency *ideally* has a specific function to perform in completing the entire task. In Nazi Germany the state attempted to handle the majority of the responsibility along–and it failed! In the United States and Canada, the Catholic Church combines its educational system with the home to perform this all-important function and has succeeded to an acceptable degree. The pragmatist would certainly not agree with much of the Catholic instructional methodology and curriculum content. He or she would tend to place the major responsibility on the public schools and the home. Many under the progressive banner may well believe that the church has a definite task to fulfill in educating what is called the student's "spiritual nature," but the pragmatist can visualize this function being successfully performed by the ideal school. The public schools in both Canada and the United States have seemingly abrogated most of their responsibility for the inculcation of so-called religious values because of controversy that would almost automatically arise.

Aims and Objectives

According to pragmatic theory, the general aim of education is more education. A mid-twentieth century pragmatist, Geiger, told us that: "education in the broadest sense can be nothing less than the changes made in human beings by their experience" (1955, Part I, p. 144). With such a fluid approach, it appears that ends become means in a continuing process as students receive experience in coping with an ever-changing environment.

To make the educational process meaningful, the necessity of an aim is self-evident. It must be mentioned that the social aim of education (broadly interpreted!) is extremely important for the pragmatic naturalist; in fact, for Dewey, social efficiency was the general aim of education. The aims and objectives that are chosen, at first undoubtedly a minority, will give the

111

individual some standards by which to set his or her course. When realized there should be no painful transition. Since life's experiences are part and parcel of the ideal pragmatic curriculum. Future aims all arise out of experience and therefore take their place naturally in people's future outlooks.

The Role of Students

The role of students in the formation of long range educational aims and immediate objectives is so important to this philosophic stance that it must be mentioned at this point—as well as under educational process. Dewey made it clear that such participation was absolutely essential in order to generate all-important, desired interest in the overall process (1938, p. 90)..

Instrumental Values

The pragmatist's ethical values cannot actually be separated from educational aims. Generally, therefore, we can say that values are instrumental for the pragmatic naturalist (i.e., subject to the purposes and circumstances of the individual. *Hence, there are no absolutely fixed values; they arise from experience!* Pupil growth, as interpreted by the pragmatist, is "all important".

Specifically, under the above-mentioned conditions, the pragmatist could subscribe to the (original) seven cardinal principles of education as published almost 100 years ago (1918) by the U. S. Bureau of Education:

(1) Health,
(2) Command of the fundamental processes,
(3) Worthy home membership,
(4) Vocational efficiency,
(5) Civic participation,
(6) Worthy use of leisure,
(7) Ethical character

Of course, these cardinal principles would be acceptable to the pragmatist *only if* the aims and objectives arose from the practical experiences of the students, parents, and teachers/ Finally pupil growth is paramount, and this

112

means that the individual is placed at the center of the educational experience.

Instructional Methodology (Educational Process)

If indeed the individual, not the subject matter, is placed at the center of the educational experience, this represents a radical revolt against all educational formalism. Here the idea of *growth* is a central one with experience playing a primary role. With this approach the teacher acts more like a guide and a counselor. Its methodology includes the use of creative projects with study units modeled after cycles of human experience. In this way thinking becomes actual problem-solving in a life experience.

The *unity of the human organism* has been accepted by most psychologists since early in the 20th century. Thus, the mind and the body should no longer be viewed as separate entities. The mind is purely and simply (although most complex!) a function of the organism. In the effort to escape the mind-body dichotomy, however, perhaps we should not take this to the opposite extreme of behaviorism.

The pragmatic naturalist seeks to discover any basic facts of the learning process. He/she wants t know its physiological and psychological bases and the laws of its operation, insofar as this is possible. We still do not have any completely tenable, adequate theory about learning from the natural and social sciences. Pragmatism will accept no truth that is not "earned" through experience.

How Learning Takes Place

The pragmatist asserts that learning takes place when interest and effort unite to produce the desired result. Effort along will produce learning of a sort, but the process se4ms much slower and more difficult. Interest of a more remote kind, such as the interests of life's aims, will usually bring effort into play when the primary tension of the first interest is slackened. Often this sort of interest tension occurs and reoccurs when a certain amount of initial learning causes both immediate and future aims to develop continually as experience progresses.

The Difficulty of Objective Evaluation

One of the most difficult problems facing modern education is determining if learning has taken place. An elaborate system of texts and measurements has been developed in an effort to solve this problem; yet, the objectivity of these tests is always open to question. The pragmatist has unusual difficulty in evaluating because, as we have seen above, his aims and objectives are likely to change as experience seems to indicate new answers. This fact leads the traditionalist to insist that the progressive has only a house built on sand. The latter counterattacks with the statement that life takes place in exactly this manner; for him, education is life. and the individual learns what he experiences. It would seem that objective evaluation is only within the realm of possibility if the judge is able to determine a person's adjustment to the environment accurately.

Knowledge is the result of a process of thought with a useful purpose. Truth is not only to be tested by its correspondence with reality, but also by its practical results. Knowledge is earned through experience and is an instrument of verification. Mind has evolved in the natural order as a more flexible means whereby people adapt themselves to the world. Learning takes place when interest and effort unite to produce the desired result. A psychological order of learning (problem-solving as explained through scientific method) is ultimately more useful than a logical arrangement proceeding from the simple fact to the complex conclusion. However, we shouldn't forget that there is always a social context to learning, and the curriculum itself should be adapted to the particular society for which it is intended.

Activity Is Necessary for Learning

The pragmatist believes that true learning takes place only when activity is involved. The emphasis should be upon directing and guiding the seemingly boundless energy of the child. Improvement is sought by building the curriculum around the basic assumption of biological activity. Effective adaptations are made daily to the many environmental problems that arise. The pragmatist tries to discover the method and conditions that favor these adaptations. The learning process is very complex. Human beings try to fulfill certain basic wants in order to achieve satisfactions; however, learning may not always accrues from this satisfied condition. If a learner has a certain amount of success with a particular method or technique, he or she may not be willing to try something new.

Mind Is a Function

Mind is viewed by the pragmatist as a function rather than as a separate structure. Hence, teaching becomes a conditioning process partially. Yet we all know that there seems to be more to the total process. The pragmatist argues that the mind tries to reach out to make its own knowledge from experience. However, the actual learning process is enigmatic. The ability of mind to react to a complicated stimulus and to make it part of the learner's own knowledge is amazing. It seems certain that this involves more than just mere imitation, or more than just a conditioned reflex. Concept formation seems to take place through some unique power of the mind when a synthesis of the new and old occurs. Interestingly, each school of thought in psychology arrives at this idea of concept formation in a different manner. Mind, a relative newcomer to the world scene, helps the pragmatist adapt to the world. Thus, the pragmatist is wary about accepting the stimulus-response description of human behavior and learning, because this might seem to indicate that a person has no creative capacity.

Answers Come Only After Participation

Pragmatism recognizes that the doctrine of the conditioned response has assumed an important place in the field of education. but he isn't to happy about it. Most educators seem to feel that it is their role to give *the* answers concerning life's problems to their students. The pragmatist would be quick to point out that such teachers are forgetting that understanding and true learning result from actual participation in the process of problem-solving. This "learning by doing" argument has been called the activity theory of learning, and it has been recognized as a very important contribution of pragmatism. This theory argues that true learning is an active and not a passive matter. We find in this approach recognition of the human's biological nature. The child learns when he/she gets first-hand. active experience in that which he wants to accomplish. By experimenting with various tentative hypotheses, we can learn through verification of the correct approach to a problem. As a result of such activity, there may be an actual change in the particular environment under consideration. Furthermore, there is an answer to those who state that some subjects such as history are not learned through activity. To this the pragmatist would agree that some types of learning may not be immediately practical, but such scientific knowledge was probably gleaned from earlier experience that was essentially most practical in nature.

Importance of Environmental Adaptation

The pragmatist emphasizes that organic behavior is characterized by responses that help the individual adapt to his environment. A person holding this position believes that reflective thinking is a sequential and ordered process that progresses toward problem solution. As blocks hinder the progress, the individual, conscious of the process taking place, makes adjustments to create more efficient means of realizing evolving goals—goals that are always tentative in the light of future experience. Most modern psychologists today emphasize the need for active involvement on the part of the learner in his or her own experience. Thus, it does seem that a gradual shift should emerge (i.e., toward the placing of the individual at the center of the educational process).

There are, of course, a number of different theories as to how learning takes place. We recognize that many factors influence learning, no matter how the process is conceived. Some of these factors are:

1. whole-and-part method,
2. transfer of training,
3. the learning curve,
4. the conditioned reflex,
5. inhibition,
6. behavior and past experience,
7. over learning of motor skills,
8. distribution of practice periods,
9. motivated learning, and
10. confidence.

All are deemed worthy of careful consideration. In this mixture where one is confronted conflicting evidence and opinions, some people find it simple to be consistently eclectic in their approach, taking what are considered to be acceptable beliefs from the various schools of thought and employing them "reasonably" in an effort to make a seeming proportionate body of thought. Despite the apparent ease and seeming attractiveness of such a "smorgasbord approach", I have never felt comfortable doing this, and I have stressed that it was philosophically indefensible to do so. I have consistently felt a strong urge to be as consistent as possible. Hence, I would encourage all others, no matter to which philosophic stance they accept, to "hang in there" until such rime as they feel compelled to switch their opinion in this respect. I have always believed that a person would be a better leader and teacher if people knew *generally* where he or she "stood" and what to expect when problems or conflicting situations arose. This is not to say, of course, that we should expect–and get!–a knee-jerk response from an intelligent teacher/administrator when a controversial matter arises...

Why I Recommend Liberal Education

North Americans should decide to what extent the traditional conception of a liberal education still holds meaning and should possibly apply for the 21st century. This concept came originally from ancient Greece, but underwent successive modifications during the periods of the Roman Empire, the medieval church, the Renaissance, and the Reformation. There was a gradual evolution of a prescribed curriculum that became a "necessary prerequisite" for the "B.A." (bachelor of arts degree), the traditional mark of a liberally educated man (sic).

As the Greeks lost their political liberty to Rome, the educated Greek was no longer a "man of action." Political expediency had actually forced him to become contemplative. Much later, when Rome had eventually fallen, at the beginning of the Middle Ages the liberal arts had been formalized and condensed from the broader Greek heritage into small literary packets of knowledge suitable only to intellectual and "spiritual" affairs. *"Material life" was largely excluded from consideration.*

With the advent of Scholasticism and the medieval universities, the liberal arts curriculum was again expanded. Specialization grew in the form of the studies of law, medicine, theology, and philosophy. The idea of a prescribed curriculum was basic, because the Church wanted clergymen and teachers to be orthodox in every respect.

The Renaissance added the study of Classical Civilization to the prescribed studies. It was at this time that secularism made an inroad into the traditional curriculum. The union of the "knightly" and the "humanistic" in the court schools of Italy was characterized by a training in arms and letters, both of which held places of distinction in the higher education of the time. Subsequently, the Reformation, with its emphasis on teaching people to read the vernacular, struck a vital blow in favor of the trend toward somewhat more democratic education.

A struggle between "culture" and "utility" has characterized curriculum development to the present day. Most educators will agree that it would be appropriate ethically for every child to achieve his or her optimum development. In the United States, for example, each child is promised "that all men are created equal; that they are endowed with certain inalienable rights; that among these are life, liberty, liberty, and the pursuit of happiness." The unfortunate reality is that world peace and unlimited economic surplus are necessary to achieve this ideal state of affairs.

At mid-20th century, the United States was still seeking to lead the Western world in a type of sociological experiment to determine whether the concept of "life, liberty, and the pursuit of happiness" was to prevail over Communistic ideology. This experiment was successful in that the former Union of Soviet Socialistic Republics was broken up. However, China and certain other countries have retained Communistic ideology while adapting to the global economy with its capitalistic roots.

The traditional purpose of a liberal arts education was viewed as the development of an ability to analyze and discriminate value. This is not being met sufficiently today in the face of educational experiences focused more on vocational development. It is argued that traditional liberal arts education is discriminatory in that it appears to be an "aristocratic pattern of education" for the intellectually elite members of society. Of course, any successful attempt at a democratic way of life makes necessary universal education for all. Within such a universal education pattern, all people should therefore be able to analyze and discriminate value successfully.

In the area of general education, the overall function should be to educate the individual as an enlightened person and cultured citizen in an evolving democracy. To become specific, *one problem to be met* by the student would be to participate in the social, economic, and political life of his/her community, state, nation, and world. A *selected competency* needed by this student to meet one aspect of this problem would be the need to appreciate the rights and responsibilities of the various racial and religious groups. The student should therefore have *a selected experience* whereby he/she would have an opportunity to attack discrimination and to work for the elimination of unfair practice. In this respect, then, several courses in the social sciences would serve as *resource areas* for the resolution of *the problem to be solved*. If such a *problem-solving approach* were used in general education, it could also be used effectively in professional education, as well as in liberal arts education. The sciences do very nicely with problem-solving experiences, of course.

Selection 8
Finding an Approach to Ethical Decision-Making

Almost everywhere one turns—as I sought to explain in the previous chapter—there is a crisis in human values as we move along in the 21st century. Because of this evident truth, I believe that the most persistent problem that any mature person faces, is the necessity for the ongoing determination (or reaffirmation) of his or her personal values. In any effort to think clearly about the matter, I believe that we may reasonably argue that there are three categories into which these values may be divided:

First, those that are ***personal*** in the sense that they relates to our immediate relations with family and friends--and our everyday life.

Secondly, as we become professionals in some field of endeavor, we should also explicitly determine our ***professional*** value orientation as a fundamental aspect of our relationship to the clients that we serve.

Thirdly, because of the way the world seems to be going, we are faced with the determination of our ***social*** or ***environmental*** values. The world is becoming ever more precarious--and "it's getting real scary out there!"

All of this is not a simple matter to resolve. People were confused and uncertain in this regard, but often they may not recognize or accept the fact that they are confused. They simply had not worked out a coherent, consistent, and reasonably logical approach to the values that they held in life. Most people simply can't express what it was they are working toward in their lives.

The values that they hold had been achieved *implicitly* and "accidentally" along the way. Typically they have simply been handed down as someone's or some organization's position, creed, or purpose. Only in rare instances has an opportunity been provided to think this subject through carefully and systematically so that an *explicitly* determined set of values was the result.

In earlier books, *Who Knows What's Right Anymore?* (2002) and *Whatever Happened to "the Good Life?"* (2003), I strove to get to the heart of this massive problem in different ways. I argued that, for several reasons, the child and the adolescent in society today are missing out almost completely on a sound "experiential" introduction to ethics. I believe this has created what I call an "ethical decision-making dilemma."

As individuals, we need to reconsider our values periodically, and then restate then in some type of graduated or hierarchical order (i.e., exactly what we believe they are in light of the changing times), and then, finally, we will then need to assess more carefully--on a regular basis—to see whether we are living up to those values we have chosen and then so often glibly espouse as well.

I believe such determination is important and desirable whether we are referring to what takes place in the home, the school system, the church, or out in the world. The truth is that typically no systematic instruction in this most important aspect of life is offered at any time. (And I refuse to accept the often-heard "osmosis stance"--that such knowledge is "better caught than taught.") It helps to have people around you who are setting good examples. However, *in the final analysis it's the individual who makes judgments and decisions based on experiences undergone.*

How Have Values Been Viewed Historically?

Socrates is typically given credit for the beginning development of Western-world standards when he considered the qualities of goodness, justice, and virtue. Then Plato gave a sort of spiritual orientation to such thought believing that these qualities were timeless (i.e., ideals (?) in a world beyond the ken of humans.

It was Plato's student, Aristotle, however who conversely searched for the answers to these matters here on Earth—here in what were early on called the "natural sciences." Then surprisingly—but interestingly—St. Thomas Aquinas picked up on Aristotle's work b giving it a spiritual dimension. Thereby he gave the human being a third dimension over and above those of mind and body. Historically it developed thereafter that the Catholic Church have related closely to Aristotle, whereas unsurprisingly Protestants identified more with Plato.

After the ancient Greeks, ethical thought was oriented more t practice than to theory. The meaning of ethical terms and concepts did not change appreciably until the marked social change of the sixteenth and seventeenth centuries in the West. At that point it was argued that ethics should be contrasted with science because the latter was presumably ethically neutral (i.e., value free). Thereafter began the continuing struggle between utilitarianism and idealism (i.e., the attempt to distinguish between what might be termed naturalistic ethics and moral law–the latter possibly prescribed by some power greater than humans.

If asked why it is so important that people give consideration to the topic of values in their lives, the answer would assuredly be that values are the major social forces that help people determine the direction culture will take at any given moment. Choices made are necessarily based on the values and norms of the culture in which people live. Such values as social values, educational values, scientific values, artistic values, etc. make up the highest level of the social system in a culture.

These values represent the "ideal general character" (e.g., social-structured facilitation of individual achievement, equality of opportunity). Remember that overall culture in itself also serves a "pattern-maintenance function" as a society confronts the ongoing functional problems it faces. Further, the values people hold have a direct relationship to how the nature of the human being is conceived.

A number of attempts have been made to define human nature on a rough historical time scale. For example, the human has been conceived in five different ways in historical progression as

> (1) a rational animal,
> (2) a spiritual being,
> (3) a receptacle of knowledge,
> (4) a mind that can be trained by exercise, and
> (5) a problem-solving organism (Morris, 1956).

Likewise, Burleson and Steiner (1964) traced six behavioral-science images of man and woman throughout recorded history. These were identified chronologically as the (1) a philosophical image, (2) a Christian image, (3) a political image, (4) an economic image, (5) a psychoanalytic image, and (6) a behavioral- science image.

How Has This "Persistent Problem" Been Handled?

As explained previously, rapid change in society had caused general confusion about the subject of ethics. Instead of having an impossible ideal confronting the practical necessity of daily life, we have such a diverse inheritance of ethical ways that no matter which one we choose, the others are at least to some degree betrayed. Obviously, this confusion has been exacerbated because of the complex of moral systems that we have inherited (e.g., Hebraic, Christian, Renaissance, Industrial--and now Islam too, for example).

This philosophic/religious confusion has historically carried over into all aspects of life. Today, it may well be impossible to gain objectivity and true historical perspective on the rapid change that is taking place. Nevertheless, a seemingly unprecedented burden of increasing complexity has been imposed on people's understanding of themselves and their world. Many leaders, along with the rest of us, must certainly be wondering whether the whole affair can be managed.

Further, as we now comprehend that the 20th century was indeed one of marked transition from one era to another, some scholars are beginning to understand that America's quite blind philosophy of optimism about history's malleability and compatibility in keeping with North American ideals may turn out to be very shortsighted. At least the weapons stalemate between the U.S.A. and the former U.S.S.R. brought to prominence the importance of nonmilitary determinants (e.g., politics and ideologies). This fact has--and also has **not**--sunk into the world's mentality. Most importantly, the world is witnessing the gradual, but seemingly inevitable, development of a vast ecological crisis that threatens the very existence of the planet known as Earth.

Can the World Turn to Philosophy for Help?

There was a time when the Western world could turn to the discipline of philosophy for guidance in regard to the question of values in the Western world. Here could be found the philosophical stance known as idealism that explained that the order of the world is due to the manifestation in space and time of an eternal and spiritual reality. Specific tenets could be subsumed under this position, as they could under the other historic philosophic position known as realism that is accepted by the Catholic Church. In contrast to these positions was the only major philosophic stance devised by humans on the North American side of the Atlantic Ocean. This position became known as pragmatism. In it nature was viewed as an emergent evolution, and the human's frame of reality is limited to nature as it functions. Here the world is characterized by activity and change, an entity on which rational man and woman have developed through organic evolution over millions of years. This world is yet incomplete--a reality that is constantly undergoing change because of a theory of emergent novelty that appears to be operating within the universe. In addition, people enjoy true freedom of will, and such freedom is achieved through continuous and developmental learning from experience.

For many years I have felt that the business of philosophy was to provide a system of ideas—to use the common parlance—that will make an integrated whole of our beliefs about the nature of the world and the values in it that will help us to fulfill our evolving human nature. Hence I accepted this so-called pragmatic maxim that avowed: "the truth or falsehood of a proposition is important only if it has some concrete bearing on the conduct of life for the individual or group. This statement has been around so long that I don't remember who it was that first defined morality as "a method of integrating (human) impulse and (social) intelligence… However, it all goes back to Dewey, Pierce, and James.

Ethical Decision-Making: A Personal Dilemma

A reasonably intelligent person today understands that most of the world's nations have won a recognizable semblance of victory over what is often a harsh physical environment. Yet many of the world's peoples living within these nations' boundaries have not yet been able to remove much of the insecurity evident in their efforts to live together constructively and peacefully. Why is this so? The "questioning" title (i.e., "Who Knows What's Right Anymore?") of my 2002 book opens the door to the fractionating division that exists in the world. The awesome power exerted by the "inherent" ethical systems of the world's organized religions needs to be fully adapted to the present before the situation can be improved.

Organized religion has continued for millennia as a social force that almost automatically controls the lives of billions of people of the world to a greater or lesser extent. One might argue that this is a good thing, that humankind truly needs the guidance provided by, for example, the "original-sin group" (i.e., the promulgators and adherents of many of the more conservative elements of the world's 13 great religions, along with the innumerable sects within these enterprises). Indeed the need for this "guidance" appears to have been vital in the distant past. It could be argued further that there is evidence that similar conditions still exist today--but to varying degrees

A second group is increasing in number daily. This second group believes that the "great" religions have had their day, and that humankind had best devise a more effective and efficient way to decide what is right and good in contrast to what is wrong and evil, respectively. This could well be called the "scientific-ethics group."

Finally, there is another truly substantive group of humans--many who are nominal members of one of the 13 (or more!) religions mentioned above--who typically live their lives as though these major religions don't even exist. This is what I am identifying loosely as the "common-sense group."

Ethical Decision-Making: A Provocative Subject

Deciding what is right and good can indeed be a most provocative subject. When you get right down to it, the "trichotomy" of "original sin or scientific ethics or common sense" is a capsule analysis of the basic choices that the majority of humankind is facing. On the one hand, there are those who believe that some external power, God or whatever, made this basic decision about right and wrong--good and evil--for humankind eons ago. On the other hand, there are those who consider such pronouncements to be largely myth or fairy tale. The latter group argues that it is up to us today to create our own "heaven and/or hell." This is to be done presumably through a steady, evolutionary, scientific search for what is good (workable) and what is bad (unworkable) or what is right or wrong. A third group, perhaps the majority of the world's population, don't really spend much time worrying about it all. When an ethical problem arises, they use their common sense (and emotion!) to arrive at a solution and then typically "muddle their way through."

Consequently, as a result of this "original sin," "scientific ethics," or "common sense" plight, people of all ages and backgrounds in most societies still find significant disagreement on the subject of human values, morality, and ethics. Nevertheless, there is also substantial evidence that many men and women are diligently and resolutely seeking a sensitive understanding of themselves and their fellows. Yet, as a result of the most divisive, long-standing, basic intra- and intercultural differences in belief that prevail, there is reason to believe that the future of the world society may well be in danger as the 21st century progresses.

Indeed, it may well be that our "distorting emotions and destructive passions" created by these and other seemingly unlovable differences represent the "greatest danger" for the future (Burtt (1965, p. 311). If such a danger does indeed exist, the development and application of a sound, but not too complex, approach to cross-cultural, ethical decision-making in personal and professional living could be of inestimable assistance to people everywhere. This will not occur, however, unless the present inability to shed many archaic beliefs and ideologies is overcome.

No Universal Foundation Available

Unfortunately, even though many philosophers have searched persistently throughout history for a normative (i.e., standard) ethical system on which people could and should base their conduct, there is still no single, non-controversial foundation accepted universally on which the entire structure of ethics can be based. This need for an acceptable, workable ethical approach is especially true at a time when developments in the field of communications, for example, have thrust us into a situation where the concept of the world as a "global village" has become a reality in the developed world. Any event that is newsworthy becomes almost immediately available through satellite communication to television stations at all points of the globe. As a result, it is becoming increasingly difficult, if not impossible, to view humanity as only an indistinct amalgam of separate cultures able to proceed in their separate ways.

Despite the above, we have witnessed a steadily rising tide of often unreasonably chauvinistic nationalism in recent years throughout the world. This development has been occasioned by an evident need for people to retain strong cultural identities through independent national status. However, because of an accompanying tide of rising expectations, we find many people within these nations--many of dubious political status--becoming part of disenfranchised populations where strife and revolt often prevail. As a result a certain percentage of these men, women, and children are seeking to move where they believe they and their offspring will have a better opportunity for "the good life.'

This turmoil in both developed and/or underdeveloped nations has created serious problems for the world, at large. Of course, this holds true, also, for America, Canada, and (now) Mexico here in our North American culture. On this side of the Atlantic, we were supposedly entering an age of leisure in the industrialized world in the 1960s, but today there's a completely different outlook confronting us as we struggle in the throes of emergence as post-industrial nations. Resultantly, this continent is rapidly becoming a vast multi-ethnic culture peopled by individuals who as they came here originally brought with them religious and ethical backgrounds. It would be too visionary, of course, to expect that cultural differentiation would cease tomorrow, and that overnight all would become enthusiastic Americans or Canadians, or Mexicans, respectively. However, it should be possible to work in that direction specifically in a much better manner than we find today.

In addition, it does bring home the need to promote steadily improving international relations. Whether the "global village" concept working in certain aspects of society (e.g., economics) will lead to the eventual establishment of one "recognizable" world culture is anybody's guess. However, cross-cultural understanding must be cultivated with great diligence. I believe this is vital because our "global village" with its blanketing communications network is steadily and inevitably viewing human values, ethics, and morality in at least a similar manner. This could well be the only hope for human civilization on Earth if people are to live together peacefully in the future.

Further, as if the need for such "harmonization" will not be difficult enough in itself, we are at present also witnessing the origins of a new science called evolutionary psychology. This developing field, based on the investigations of evolutionary biologists and a variety of social-science scholars, presents a strong possibility (probability?) that the end result will be a sharply revised view of human nature itself. Assessing contemporary social reality, Wright (1994) argues that a new understanding of the imperatives required by human genes is needed. Resultantly, it could be that the very foundation of our human concept of goodness will never be the same again.

With thoughts such as these as a backdrop, I have personally "survived" as a presumably ethical, dual citizen of Canada and America, a person who has worked professionally for a total of 70 years in both countries (first one, then the other, etc.). Yet I have also long since come to the conclusion that we all face a confusing "Tower of Babel" daily when we are confronted with everyday decision-making about problems of an ethical nature. I say this because in our relationships with others we so often seem to be speaking "different languages" about what's right and what's wrong, as well as which actions are good and which are bad.

I have found this statement to be true for many reasons: whether a parent is speaking to a son or daughter about a social-relationship problem in school, whether that same parent is facing a marital problem in the home, whether a member of that family confronts someone with an issue on a neighborhood street, or whether the same man or woman has an ethical decision to make at work as a professional practitioner or tradesperson. Let's face it, these examples cited just scratch the surface of the many issues and concerns about which the individual is required to make rapid decisions daily.

A "Down-to-Earth" Approach to Ethics

Seeking to improve what basically amounts to a "cultural impasse," in this book I can only offer you what I believe to be a down-to-earth approach looking to the resolution of the many personal, social/environmental, and professional problems facing us all from one day to the next. I must confess immediately that I have strayed completely from the stated or implied "religious ethics" of my upbringing as a Protestant (Lutheran, Baptist, and agnostic Unitarian-Universalist in that order). Over time I have found present in me a strong, steadily growing belief that we (all people in the developing world) must somehow--and relatively soon--rise above this or that sectarian religious or ideological position. As the world is turning, indeed we must--if we ever hope to have a peaceful world--seek a workable level of normative consensus among the conflicting ethical beliefs of the world's leading religions and ideologies.

Trained philosophers, especially those of the "analytic persuasion"* may well view this practical approach as reductionistic (i.e., abridged and overly simplified). Such an assessment would only be true to a degree, since the first phase of this approach to ethical decision-making should not be new or antithetical to them. In fact, it is a well-considered plan that one of the persons to whom I am indebted for this approach (Dr. Richard Fox of Cleveland State University) used for many years with college undergraduates. He did so because he felt that an elementary, straightforward plan at least got reasonably intelligent students off to a good start with the subject of applied ethics. Of course, how they subsequently approached ethical decision-making as they matured could well be another matter.

So, if you will grant what I stated originally above as an apparent truth--i.e., the moral confusion that prevails currently in North America and elsewhere in much of the world--I will assume further that all who read these words will be interested also in improving society's educational process in this aspect of general education. Basically, I am arguing that all children and young people in our society should have the opportunity to develop their own rational powers through the finest possible, competency-based educational experience relating to ethics and morality. (I might add that I am not for a minute recommending any retroactive change in the basic separation of church and state where it already exists, but I do believe that some agreement regarding the subject-matter of ethics and morality, as well as about an appropriate, accompanying teaching methodology, is needed urgently so that this subject may be taught within public education at all levels.)

Any new approach being recommended needs solid justification. I believe strongly that such a case can be made for the approach recommended here for North America--as a point of departure. In the first place, I have tried it out personally and professionally over a period of many years in class with my own university students, and it worked very well basically. Experience indicated where certain modifications were advisable, and these changes were made and have also been incorporated here.

Secondly, I want to make clear that no effort will be made to indoctrinate you, the reader, to accept any one of the numerous approaches to ethical decision-making that are available in the Western world today. Yet I do recommend here initially one approach (a three-step one) of a normative nature for experimentation because it is quite consistent with the historical values and norms of North American society to this point. However I make it crystal-clear, also, that each person should, in the final analysis, work this out for himself or herself. (This seems only fair since sensitive understanding in essential to treat a subject that is undoubtedly highly controversial and taught "at one's peril" presently in public education.)

In the experiential educational process recommended here, the hope is that reason will begin to act as the programmer of a person's "emotional computer" as soon as possible in his or her life. Our primary concern as parents or teachers should, also, be to help the boy or girl to develop conscious convictions in which the mind leads and the emotions follow. In this way the maturing person would gradually learn what values are important to him or to her. As Ayn Rand (1960) explained, "the integrated sum of a person's basic values is that person's sense of life" (p. 35).

To cite one important example where improved ethical decision-making is needed, permit me to describe a subject that I know very well, competitive sport. It has become increasingly apparent to me that there is an urgent need for those involved in highly competitive sport to understand and then to develop a greatly improved approach to sport ethics and morality. Social institutions (e.g., religion, economics, education) are presumed to be beneficial to society as a whole--not detrimental! Yet as I see it, if we expect beneficial transfer of training to occur, highly competitive sport as a social institution may currently be doing more harm than good in the promotion of *sound* human relations and development. (This assertion is made about sport at the "upper" levels of higher education and professional sport in the United States especially, but it undoubted applies to professional sport everywhere).

Thus, because of what I have assessed as a steadily deteriorating situation in U.S. competitive sport, I strongly believe that the development of a proper understanding of the prevailing "immoral" situation in U.S. is very important for athletes, coaches, athletic administrators, game officials, teachers, students, educational administrators, governing board members, local citizens, state or provincial legislators, and all the citizens of the nation. As I see it, also, a farsighted plan should be developed first from the standpoint of the possible contribution of ethical instruction to the general education of young people who may strive to be athletes in society. In addition, it should be developed insofar as this subject might be introduced as a requirement into professional preparation programs in which coaches and physical educators are trained.

The Young Person's "Sense of Life"

Bringing this discussion back to the developing young person and a general education perspective, consider this analysis of what occurs before any semblance of a rational philosophy develops. In this analogy, offered by Ayn Rand, she delineates first the youthful human's possession of a "psychological recorder," that which is truly the person's inherent subconscious, integrating mechanism. This so-called sense of life she views as "a pre-conceptual equivalent of metaphysics, an emotional, subconsciously integrated appraisal of man and existence." As she sees it, this determines "the nature of a man's emotional responses and the essence of his character" (p. 31).

So what the young person really needs at this juncture of his or her development, she explains further, is an "intellectual roadbed" that provides a "course of life" to follow. The eventual goal should be a fully integrated personality, a person whose mind and emotions are in harmony a great deal of the time. When this occurs, we find a situation where the individual's sense of life matches his or her conscious convictions. It is fundamental further, of course, that the young person's view of reality be carefully defined by himself or herself and is reasonably consistent. And, the argument continues, if ethical instruction was planned more carefully and explicitly, the quality of living would probably be greatly improved for all.

As I believe it is happening today in North America, we have been led, most unfortunately, to the point where the child or young person typically learns to make rational ethical decisions poorly and inadequately. I strongly believe that this is a tragic condition because the young person's all-important personality development is so often misdirected, misguided, and at least temporarily stunted.

Concluding Statement

In summary, I have argued here that we require a steadily improving crop of young citizens and professional people whose general education and professional education is under girded by sound theory based on solid research and scholarly endeavor. Moreover, and perhaps more important ultimately, I have argued further that all of this will be in vain if we do not turn out high-caliber young people with high ethical standards. Accordingly, we are faced with the urgent need to make certain that such ethical sensitivity will be attained as a required competency by those students who emerge from our educational system.

So there it is. Recognizing and appreciating that values, ethics, and morality are a vital part of our heritage, present living, and our future, I hope that you, the reader, will be helped by this volume to forge an improved personal and professional approach to ethical decision-making in your life. I hope you have read and assessed this introductory section carefully. Keep in mind Anderson's admonition ((1997, p. 155) that "all ethical and moral systems are created by people, and by people as they are at a certain time and place."

References

Anderson, W. T. (1997) *The future of the self.* NY: Penguin Putnam.
Rand, A. (1960). *The romantic manifesto.* NY & Cleveland: World.
Wright, R. (1994) *The moral animal.* NY: Pantheon.

Selection 9
Counteracting America's Value Orientation
Via Postmodernism

The term *"modernism"* is used typically to describe cultural movements in today's world that were caused by onrushing science, technology, and economic globalization. It is said to have started in the late nineteenth and early twentieth century. Conversely, *postmodernism*, as variously defined, can be described loosely as an effort by some intelligent and possibly wise people to react against what is happening to this *modern* world as it "races headlong" toward an indeterminate future. Although I've been grumbling about the term "postmodern" for years, nevertheless I now believe that we are all being *forced* to grapple with the concept. Yet, if we do, I can't help but feel that the encounter brings to mind the story of the blind man asked to describe an elephant while holding its tail.

Unfortunately, the term postmodernism has become as badly garbled as have the terms existentialism, pragmatism, idealism, etc. The result is that postmodernism is now used loosely by many and only occasionally by the few truly seeking to analyze what may have been the intent of those who coined the term in the first place. I recall an earlier discussion group where the question of the hour was: "What does the term "postmodernism" mean to you?" I left the discussion early on because I found that there was no initial definition of the term with which to begin the discussion. In some instances today, we are receiving seemingly deliberate obfuscation by people evidently trying to "fool the public." As I see it, if anything's worth saying, it must be said as carefully and understandably as possible. Otherwise one can't help but think that the speaker (or writer) is either deceitful, confused, or prejudiced.

What to do? First, before going any further, I think we need to look at the world situation today. If what we find may be called **modernism,** then what is this **"postmodernism"** that has arisen as a protest or "counter-ideology" to improve what is obviously a world "in need of repair." It can be argued reasonably that America's thrust is modernistic to the nth degree. To the extent that this is true, I am arguing here conversely that Canada should work to counteract America's value orientation as the world moves along in the 21st century. I believe that Canada can--and should do this--by adopting a position that might be called "moderate" postmodernism.

Granted that it will be most difficult for Canada to consistently exhibit a different "thrust" than its neighbor to the south. Nevertheless I believe that now is the time for Canada to deliberately create a society characterized by the better elements of what has been termed postmodernism. In fact, I feel Canadians will be *forced* to grapple with the basic thrust of modernism in the 21st century if they hope to avoid the "twilight" that is descending on "American culture" (Berman, 2000). You, the reader, may well question this stark statement about our immediate neighbor. However, bear with me, and let us begin.

What is postmodernism? While most philosophers have been "elsewhere engaged" for the past 50 plus years, what has been called postmodernism, and what I believe is poorly defined for the edification of most, has gradually become a substantive factor in broader intellectual circles. I freely admit to have been grumbling about the term "postmodern" for decades. I say this because somehow it too has been used badly as have other philosophic terms such as existentialism, pragmatism, idealism, realism, etc. as they emerged to become common parlance.

In this ongoing process, postmodernism was often used by a minority to challenge prevailing knowledge, and considerably less by the few truly seeking to analyze what was the intent of those who coined the term originally. For example, I am personally not suggesting, as some have, that scientific evidence and empirical reasoning are to be taken with a grain of salt based on someone's subjective reality. Further, if anything is worth saying, I believe it should be said as carefully and understandably as possible. Accordingly, the terms used must be defined, at least tentatively. Otherwise one can't help but think that the speaker (or writer) is either deceitful, a confused person, or has an axe to grind.

If nothing in the world is absolute, and one value is as good as another in a world increasingly threatened with collapse and impending doom, as some say postmodernists claim, then one idea is possibly as good as another in any search to cope with the planet's myriad problems. This caricature of a postmodern world, as one in which we can avoid dealing with the harsh realities facing humankind, is hardly what any rational person might suggest. How can humankind choose to avoid (1) looming environmental disaster, (2) ongoing war because of daily terrorist threats, and (3) hordes of displaced, starving people, many of whom are now victims of conflicts within troubled cultures? Further, as we still occasionally hear said, *what rational being would argue that one idea is really as good as another?*

What then is humankind to do in the face of the present confusion and conflicted assertions about postmodernism from several quarters that have been circulated? First, I think we need to analyze the world situation very carefully. Perhaps this will provide us with a snapshot of the milieu where we can at least see the need for a changing (or changed) perspective that would cause humankind to abandon the eventual, destructive elements of modernism that threaten us. An initial look at some of the developments of the second half of the twentieth century may provide a perspective from which to judge the situation.

Historical Perspective on the "World Situation"

In this analysis of the present situation, after the introductory statement the following topics will be considered in the ordered listed below:

1. Introduction
2. Historical Perspective on the "World Situation"
3. America's Position in the 21st Century
4. The Impact of Negative Social Forces Has Increased.
5. What Character Do We Seek for People?
6. What Happened to the Original Enlightenment Ideal?
7. Future Societal Scenarios (Anderson)
8. What Kind of A World Do You Want for Your Descendents?
9. Can We Strengthen the Postmodern Influence?
10. Concluding Statement

In this search for historical perspective on world society today, we need to keep in mind the significant developments of the decades immediately preceding the turn of the 21st century. For example, Naisbitt (1982) outlined the "ten new directions that are transforming our lives." Then his wife and he suggested the "megatrends" they saw insofar as women's evolving role in the societal structure (Aburdene & Naisbitt, 1992). Here I refer to:

1. The concepts of the information society and

Internet,
2. "High tech/high touch,"
3. The shift to world economy,
4. The need to shift to long-term thinking in regard to ecology,
5. The move toward organizational decentralization,
6. The trend toward self-help,
7, The ongoing discussion of the wisdom of participatory democracy as opposed to representative democracy,
8. A shift toward networking,
9. A reconsideration of the "north-south" orientation, and
10. The viewing of decisions as "multiple option" instead of "either/or."

Add to this the ever-increasing, lifelong involvement of women in the workplace, politics, sports, organized religion, and social activism. Now, we can begin to understand that a new world order has descended upon us as we begin the 21st century.

Just after Naisbitt's first set of *Megatrends* appeared, a second list of 10 issues facing political leaders was highlighted in the *Utne Reader*. It was titled "Ten events that shook the world between 1984 and 1994" (1994, pp. 58-74). Consider the following:

1. the fall of communism and the continuing rise of nationalism,
2. the environmental crisis and the Green movement,
3. the AIDS epidemic and the "gay response,"
4. continuing wars (29 in 1993) and the peace movement,
5. the gender war,
6. religion and racial tension,
7. the concept of "West meets East" and resultant implications,
8. the "Baby Boomers" came of age and "Generation X" has started to worry and complain because of declining expectation levels,
9. the whole idea of "globalism" and international markets, and
10. the computer revolution and the specter of the Internet.

It is true that the world's "economic manageability"—or adaptability to cope with such change-–may have been helped by its division into three major trading blocs:

1. the Pacific Rim long dominated by Japan [and now by China as well];
2. the European Community very heavily influenced by Germany; and
3. North America dominated by the United States of America.

While this appears to be true to some observers, interestingly perhaps something even more fundamental has occurred. Succinctly put, world politics seems to be "entering a new phase in which the fundamental source of conflict will be neither ideological nor economic." In the place of these, Samuel P. Huntington, of Harvard's Institute for Strategic Studies, has asserted that now the major conflicts in the world would be clashes between different groups of civilizations espousing fundamentally different cultures (1998).

These clashes represent a distinct shift away from viewing the world as being composed of "first, second, and third worlds" as was the case during the Cold War. Thus, Huntington is arguing that in the 21st century the world will return to a pattern of development evident several hundred years ago in which civilizations will actually rise and fall. (Interestingly, this is exactly what the late Arnold Toynbee in his now famous theory of history development stated (1947). However, to confuse the situation even more, most recently we have been warned by scholars about the increasing number of clashes within civilizations!)

Internationally, after the dissolution of the Union of Soviet Socialist Republics (the USSR), Russia and the remaining communist regimes have been challenged severely as they sought to convert to more of a capitalistic economic system. Additionally, a number of other multinational countries are regularly showing signs of potential breakups. Further, the evidence points to the strong possibility that the developing nations are becoming ever poorer and more destitute with burgeoning populations resulting in widespread starvation caused by both social and ecological factors.

Further, Western Europe is facing a demographic time bomb even more than the United States because of the influx of refugees from African and Islamic countries, not to mention refugees from countries of the former Soviet Union. It is evident, also, that the European Community is inclined to appease Islam's demands. However, the multinational nature of the European Community will tend to bring on economic protectionism to insulate its economy against the rising costs of prevailing socialist legislation.

Still further, there is evidence that "Radical Islam," seemingly along with Communist China, is becoming increasingly aggressive toward the Western culture of Europe and North America. At present, Islam gives evidence of replacing Marxism as the world's main ideology of confrontation. For example, Islam is dedicated to regaining control of Jerusalem and to force Israel to give up control of land occupied earlier to provide a buffer zone against Arab aggressors. In addition, China has been arming certain Arab nations. Yet, how can the West be critical in this regard when we recall that the U.S.A. has also armed selected countries in the past [and present?] when such support was deemed in its interest?)

As Hong Kong, despite its ongoing protestations, is gradually absorbed into Communist China, further political problems seem inevitable in the Far East as well. Although North Korea is facing agricultural problems, there is the possibility (probability?) of the building of nuclear bombs there along with the capability to deploy them. Further, there is the ever-present fear worldwide that Iran, other smaller nations, and terrorists will somehow get nuclear weapons too. A growing Japanese assertiveness in Asian and world affairs also seems inevitable because of its typically very strong financial position. Yet the flow of foreign capital from Japan into North America has slowed down. This is probably because Japan has been confronted with its own financial crisis caused by inflated real estate and market values. Also, there would obviously be a strong reaction to any fall in living standards in this tightly knit society. Interestingly, further, the famed Japanese work ethic has become somewhat tarnished by the growing attraction of leisure opportunities.

The situation in Africa has become increasingly grim. Countries south of the Sahara Desert—that is, the dividing line between Black Africa and the Arab world—have experienced extremely bad economic performance in the past two decades. This social influence has brought to a halt much of the continental effort leading to political liberalization while at the same time exacerbating traditional ethnic rivalries. This economic problem has accordingly forced governmental cutbacks in many of the countries because of the pressures brought to bear by the financial institutions of the Western world that have been underwriting much of the development that had taken place.

> (Note: And now look at the trouble those very institutions are experiencing!) The poor are therefore getting poorer, and health and education standards have generally deteriorated even lower than they were previously. At this point one wonders how there ever was thought about the average family ever living "the good life."

America's Position in the 21st Century

Reviewing America's position in the 21st century may help us to get to the heart of the matter about where the world is heading. For example, we could argue that North Americans do not fully comprehend that their unique position in the history of the world's development will in all probability change radically for the worse in the 21st century. Actually, of course, the years ahead are really going to be difficult ones for all of the world's citizens. However, it does appear that the United States is currently setting itself up "big time" for all kinds of societal difficulties. As the one major nuclear power, Uncle Sam has taken on the ongoing, overriding problem of maintaining large-scale peace. At the turn of the 20th century Teddy Roosevelt, while "speaking softly," nevertheless had his "big stick." The George ("W") Bush administration at the beginning of the 21st century had its "big stick", also, but it hasn't given a minute's thought about "speaking softly." This president actually did claim that America's assertive actions are "under God" and are designed for the good of all humanity. This caused various countries, both large and small, to speak out about many perceive as a bullying posture. Some of these countries may or may not have nuclear arms capability already. That is what is so worrisome.

America, despite all of its proclaimed good intentions, may well find that history is going against it in several ways. This means that previous optimism may need to be tempered to shake politicians loose from delusions, some of which persist despite what seems to be commonsense logic. For example, it is troublesome that, despite the presence of the United Nations, the United States has persisted in positioning itself as the world superpower. Such posturing and aggression, often by unilateral action with the hoped-for, belated sanction of the United Nations, has resulted in the recent United States-led wars in the Middle East and other incursion into Somalia and then Afghanistan for very different reasons. There are also other similar situations on the recent horizon, and I haven't even mentioned the "Vietnam disaster" of the 1960s. Hence–let's face it (!)–who knows what the Central Intelligence Agency has been doing lately to make the world safe for American-style democracy. . .? Fidel Castro, after surviving so many assassination-attempts, can now breathe more easily as he approaches death from illness.

There may be reason, post-Obama now that is, to expect selected U.S. cutbacks brought on by today's excessive world involvement and enormous debt. It appears that many in "the World" do indeed wish President Obama well, but significant retrenchment due to financial debt will probably inevitably lead to a decline in the economic and military influence of the United States. However, who can argue logically that the present uneasy balance of power is a healthy situation looking to the future? A most important factor in the complex equation of the future is the way the human mind responds to crisis. The world culture as we know it today simply must respond adequately and peacefully to the many challenges with which it is being confronted. The societies and nations must individually and collectively respond positively, intelligently, and strongly if humanity as we have known it is to survive.

Additionally, problems and concerns of varying magnitude abound. It seems inevitable that all of the world will be having increasingly severe ecological problems, not to mention the ebbs and flows of an energy crisis. Generally, also, there is a worldwide nutritional problem, and an ongoing situation where the rising expectations of the underdeveloped nations, including their staggering debt, will have to be met somehow. These are just a few of the major concerns looming on the horizon. In addition, now we find that America has spent so much more "straightening out" the "enemy" and "helping others" that its debt has reached staggering proportions.

In his insightful analysis, *The twilight of American culture* (2000), Morris Berman explained that historically four factors are present when a civilization is threatened with collapse:

1. Accelerating social and economic inequality,
2. Declining marginal returns with regard to

investments in organizational solutions to socioeconomic problems,

3. Rapidly dropping levels of literacy, critical understanding, and general intellectual awareness, and

4. Spiritual death--that is, Spengler's classicism: the emptying out of cultural content and the freezing (or repackaging) of it in formulas--kitsch, in short. (p. 19).

He then states that all of these factors are increasingly present on the American scene. Question: how did America get itself into this presenting highly precarious situation in regard to the daily lives of its citizens?

The Impact of Negative Social Forces Has Increased.

Keeping our focus on humankind's search for "the good life" in the 21st century, in North America we are finding that the human recreational experience will have to be earned typically within a society whose very structure has been modified. For example,

1. The concept of the traditional family structure has been strongly challenged by a variety of social forces (e.g., economics, divorce rate);
2. Many single people are finding that they must work longer hours; and
3. Many families need more than one breadwinner just to make ends meet.

Also, the idea of a steady surplus economy may have vanished in the presence of a burgeoning budgetary deficit. What nonessentials do we cut from the debt-overwhelmed budget at a time like this to bring back what might be called fiscal sanity?

Additionally, many of the same problems of megalopolis living described back in the 1960s still prevail. In fact, they are even increasing (e.g., declining infrastructure, crime rates in multiethnic populated centers, transportation gridlocks, overcrowded school classrooms). Thinking back to 1967 in Canada, Prime Minister Lester Pearson asked Canadians to improve "the quality of Canadian life" as Canada celebrated her 100th anniversary as a confederation. Interestingly, still today, despite all of Canada's current identity problems, some pride can be taken in the fact that Canada has on occasion been proclaimed as the best place on earth to live. Nevertheless, we can't escape the fact that the work-week is not getting shorter and shorter, and that the predictions of the 1960s about achieving four different types of leisure class are but a distant dream for the large majority of people.

Further, the situation has developed in such a way that the presently maturing generation is finding (1) that fewer good-paying jobs are available and (2) that the average annual income is declining (especially if we keep a steadily rising cost of living in mind). What caused this to happen is not a simple question to answer. For one thing, despite the rosy picture envisioned a generation ago—one in which we were supposedly entering a new stage for humankind—we are unable today to cope adequately with the multitude of problems that have developed. This situation is true whether inner city, suburbia, exurbia, or small-town living is concerned. Transportation jams and gridlock, for example, are occurring daily as public transportation struggles to meet rising demand for economical transport within the framework of developing megalopolises.

Certainly, megalopolis living trends have not abated and will probably not do so in the predictable future. More and more families, where that unit is still present, need two breadwinners just to survive. Interest rates, although minor cuts are made when economic slowdowns occur, have been reasonable. A truly troubled real estate market now discourages many people from home ownership, as myriad others are defaulting on their mortgage liabilities. Pollution of air and water continues despite efforts of many to change the present course of development. High-wage industries seem to be "heading south" in search of places where lower wages can be paid. Also, all sorts of crime are still present in our society, a goodly portion of it seemingly brought about by unemployment, drug-taking, and rising debt at all levels from the individual to the federal government.

The continuing presence of youth crime is especially disturbing. (This is especially true when homegrown youth turn to terrorism!) In this respect, it is fortunate in North America that municipal, private-agency, and public recreation has received continuing financial support from the increasingly burdened taxpayer. Even here, however, there has been a definite trend toward user fees for many recreational services thereby affecting people's ability to get involved. Life goes on, however, but the question arises in ongoing discussions as to what character we seek for people within a burgeoning population.

What Character Do We Seek for People?

Functioning in a world that is steadily becoming a "Global Village," or a "flat earth" as described by Thomas Friedman, we need to think more seriously than ever before about the character and traits which we should seek to develop in people. Not even mentioning the Third World, people in what we call "developed nations" continue to lead or strive for the proverbial good life. To attain this state, children and young people need to develop the right attitudes (psychologically speaking) toward education, work, use of leisure, participation in government, various types of consumption, and concern for world stability and peace. If we truly desire "the good life," we somehow have to provide an increased level of education for the creative and constructive use of leisure to a greater percentage of the population. As matters stand, there doesn't seem to be much impetus in the direction of achieving this balance as a significant part of ongoing general education. We are simply not ready for a society where education for leisure has a unique role to play on into the indeterminate future. One wonders how such a development might affect the character of our young people?

What are called the "Old World countries" all seem to have a "character"; it is almost something that they take for granted. However, it is questionable whether there is anything that can be called a character in North America (i.e., in the United States? in Canada?). Americans were thought earlier to be heterogeneous and individualistic as a people, as opposed to Canadians. However, the Canadian culture—whatever that may be today! —has moved toward multiculturalism quite significantly in the past two decades. Of course, Canada was founded by two distinct cultures, the English and the French. In addition to working out a continuing, reasonably happy relationship between these two cultures, it is now a question because of an aggressive "multicultural approach" of assimilating these newcomers arriving from many different lands as *dedicated Canadians*! In addition, we must not forget the claims of "first nations" whose 99 entities in British Columbia along claim more territory than exists!

Shortly after the middle of the twentieth century, Commager (1966), the noted historian, enumerated what he believed were some common denominators in American (i.e., U.S.) character. These, he said, were:

1. carelessness;
2. openhandedness, generosity, and hospitality;
3. self-indulgence;
4. sentimentality, and even romanticism;
5. gregariousness;
6. materialism;
7. confidence and self-confidence;
8. complacency, bordering occasionally on arrogance;
8. cultivation of the competitive spirit;
9. indifference to, and exasperation with laws, rules,
    and regulations;
10. equalitarianism; and (
11. resourcefulness (pp. 246-254).

What about Canadian character as opposed to what Commager stated above for America? Although completed a quarter of a century ago, Lipset (1973) carried out a perceptive comparison between the two countries that has probably not changed significantly in the interim. He reported that these two countries probably resemble each other more than any other two in the world. Nevertheless, he asserted that there seemed to be a rather "consistent pattern of differences between them" (p. 4). He found that certain "special differences" did exist and may be singled out as follows:

Varying origins in their political systems and national identities, varying religious traditions, and varying frontier experiences. In general terms, the value orientations of Canada stem from a counterrevolutionary past, a need to differentiate itself from the United States, the influence of monarchical institutions, a dominant Anglican religious tradition, and a less individualistic and more governmentally controlled expansion of the Canadian than of the American frontier (p. 5).

Seymour Lipset's findings (1973) tended to sharpen the focus on opinions commonly held earlier that, even though there is considerable sharing of values, they are held more tentatively in Canada. Also, he believed that Canada had consistently settled on "the middle ground" between positions arrived at in the United States and England. However, Lipset argued that, although the twin values of equalitarianism and achievement have been paramount in American life--but somewhat less important in Canada--there was now consistent movement in this direction in Canada as well (p. 6). Keeping national aims, value orientations, and character traits in mind as being highly important, of course, as well all of the material progress that has been made by a segment of the population, we are nevertheless forced to ask ourselves if we in Canada are "on the right track heading in the right direction?"

What Happened to the Original Enlightenment Ideal?

The achievement of "the good life" for a majority of citizens in the developed nations, a good life that involves a creative and constructive use of leisure as a key part of general education, necessarily implies that a certain type of progress has been made in society. However, we should understand that the chief criterion of progress has undergone a subtle but decisive change since the founding of the United States republic in North America. This development has had a definite influence on Canada and Mexico as well. Such change has been at once a cause and a reflection of the current disenchantment with technology. Recall that the late 18th century was a time of political revolution when monarchies and aristocracies, and that the ecclesiastical structure were being challenged on a number of fronts in the Western world. Also, the factory system was undergoing significant change at that time.

As Leo Marx (1990, p. 5) reported such industrial development with its greatly improved machinery "coincided with the formulation and diffusion of the modern Enlightenment idea of history as a record of progress..." He explained further that this: "new scientific knowledge and accompanying technological power was expected to make possible a comprehensive improvement in all of the conditions of life—social, political, moral, and intellectual as well as material." This idea did indeed slowly take hold and eventually "became the fulcrum of the dominant American world view" (p. 5). By 1850, however, with the rapid growth of the United States especially, the idea of progress was already being dissociated from the Enlightenment vision of political and social liberation.

By the turn of the twentieth century, "the technocratic idea of progress [had become] a belief in the sufficiency of scientific and technological innovation as the basis for general progress" (Marx, p. 9). This came to mean that if scientific-based technologies were permitted to develop in an unconstrained manner, there would be an automatic improvement in all other aspects of life! What happened—because this theory became coupled with onrushing, unbridled capitalism—was that the ideal envisioned by Thomas Jefferson in the United States has been turned upside down. Instead of social progress being guided by such values as justice, freedom, and self-fulfillment for all people, rich or poor, these goals of vital interest in a democracy were subjugated to a burgeoning society dominated by supposedly more important instrumental values (i.e., useful or practical ones for advancing a capitalistic system).

Have conditions improved? The answer to this question is obvious. The fundamental question still today is, "which type of values will win out in the long run?" In North America, for example, a developing concept of cultural relativism was being discredited as the 1990s witnessed a sharp clash between (1) those who uphold so-called Western cultural values and (2) those who by their presence are dividing the West along a multitude of ethnic and racial lines. This is witnessed by strong efforts to promote "fundamentalist" religions and sects—either those present historically or those recently imported. These numerous religions, and accompanying sects, are characterized typically by decisive right/wrong morality. It is this type of "progress" that has led concerned people to inquire where we in the developed world are heading. What kind of a future is "out there" for humankind if the world continues in the same direction it is presently heading? We don't know for certain, of course, but a number of different scenarios can be envisioned depending on humanity's response to the present crisis of a society characterized by modernism.

Future Societal Scenarios (Anderson)

In this adventure of civilization, Walter Truett Anderson, then president of the American Division of the World Academy of Art and Science, postulates four different scenarios for the future of earthlings. In *The future of the self: Inventing the postmodern person* (1997), Anderson argues convincingly that current trends are adding up to an early 21st-century identity crisis for humankind. The creation of the present "modern self," he explains, began with Plato, Aristotle, and with the rights of humans in Roman legal codes.

Anderson argues that the developing conception of self bogged down in the Middle Ages, but fortunately was resurrected in the Renaissance Period of the second half of The Middle Ages. Since then the human "self" has been advancing like a "house afire" as the Western world has gone

146

through an almost unbelievable transformation. Without resorting to historical detail, I will say only that scientists like Galileo and Copernicus influenced philosophers such as Descartes and Locke to foresee a world in which the self was invested with human rights.

Anderson's "One World, Many Universes" version is prophesied as the most likely to occur. This is a scenario characterized by (1) high economic growth, (2) steadily increasing technological progress, and (3) globalization combined with high psychological development. Such psychological maturity, he predicts, will be possible for a certain segment of the world's population because "active life spans will be gradually lengthened through various advances in health maintenance and medicine" (pp. 251-253). (This scenario may seem desirable, of course, to people who are coping reasonably well at present.)

However, it appears that a problem has developed at the beginning of this new century with this dream of individual achievement of inalienable rights and privileges. The modern self–envisioned by Descartes–a rational, integrated self that Anderson likens to Captain Kirk at the command post of the original Starship Enterprise–is having an identity crisis. The image of this bold leader (he or she!) taking us fearlessly into the great unknown has begun to fade as alternate scenarios for the future of life on Earth are envisioned.

For example, John Bogle of Vanguard, in his *The Battle for the Soul of Capitalism* (2007) argues that what he terms "global capitalism" is destroying the already uneasy balance between democracy as a political system and capitalism as an economic system. In a world where globalization and economic "progress" seemingly must be rejected because of catastrophic environmental concerns or "demands," the bold-future image could well "be replaced by a postmodern self; de-centered, multidimensional, and changeable" (p. 50).

Captain Kirk, or Barack Obama now, as he "boldly goes where no man has gone before"–this time to "restore America's place in the world firmament while ridding the world of terrorists–is facing a second crucial change. As the American Government seeks to shape the world of the 21st century, based on Anderson's analysis, there is another force--the systemic-change force mentioned above--that is shaping the future. This all-powerful force may well exceed the Earth's ability to cope with what happens. As gratifying as such factors as "globalization along with economic growth" and "psychological development" may seem to the folks in Anderson's "One-World, Many Universes" scenario, there is a flip side to this prognosis. This image, Anderson identifies, as "The Dysfunctional Family" scenario. It turns out that all of the "benefits" of so-called progress are highly expensive and available now only to relatively few of the six billion plus people on earth. Anderson foresees this scenario as "a world of modern people relatively happily doing their thing—modern people still obsessed with progress, economic gain, and organizational bigness—along with varieties of postmodern people being trampled and getting angry" [italics added] (p. 51). And, I might add further, as people get angrier, the present-day threat of terrorism in North America could seem like child's play.

What Kind of A World Do You Want for Your Descendents?

What I am really asking here is whether you, the reader of these words, is cognizant of, and approves of, the situation as it is developing today. Are you (and I too!) simply "going along with the crowd" while taking the path of least resistance? Can we do anything to improve the situation by implementing an approach that could help to make the situation more beneficent and wholesome in perspective? *What I am recommending is that the time is ripe for a country like Canada to distinguish itself more aggressively as being on a "different path" than the United States of America.* To do this, however, individually and collectively, we would need to determine what sort of a world we (and our descendants) should be living in.

If you consider yourself an environmentalist, for example, the future undoubtedly looks bleak to you. What can we so to counter the strong business orientation of our society (i.e., being swept along with the "onward and upward" economic and technologic growth of American modernism)? Such is most certainly not the answer to all of our developing problems and issues. We should see ourselves increasingly as "New Agers" working to help Canada working to forge its own identity. I grant you, however, some sort of mass, non-religious "spiritual" transformation would have to take place for this to become a reality.

Let me offer one example based on my personal experience where I think Canada can make a good beginning in this respect. (Some who read this may wish to hang me in effigy [or literally!] for this assertion). Nevertheless, I believe that Canada should strive to hold back the negative

148

influences of America's approach to overly commercial, competitive sport in both universities and the public sector. At present, we are too often typically conforming blindly to a power structure in which sport is used largely by private enterprise or other interests for selfish purposes. The problem is this: opportunities for participation in all competitive sport--not just Olympic sport--moved historically from amateurism to semi-professionalism, and then on to full-blown professionalism.

The Olympic Movement, because of a variety of social pressures, followed suit in both ancient times and the present. When the International Olympic Committee gave that final push to the pendulum and openly admitted professional athletes to play in the Games, they may have pleased most of the spectators and all of the advertising and media representatives. However, in so doing the floodgates were opened completely. The original ideals upon which the Games were reactivated were completely abandoned. This is what caused Sir Rees-Mogg in Britain (20 years ago!), for example, to state that crass commercialism had won the day (1988). This final abandonment of any semblance of what was the original Olympic ideal was the "straw that broke the camel's back." This ultimate decision regarding eligibility for participation has indeed been devastating to those people who earnestly believe that money and sport are like oil and water; they simply do not mix! Their response has been to abandon any further interest in, or support for, the entire Olympic Movement.

The question must, therefore be asked: "What should rampant professionalism in competitive sport at the Olympic Games mean to any given country out of the 200-plus nations involved?" This is not a simple question to answer responsibly. In this present brief statement, it should be made clear that the professed social values of a country should ultimately prevail--and that they will prevail in the final analysis. However, this ultimate determination will not take place overnight. The fundamental social values of a social system will eventually have a strong influence on the individual values held by most citizens in that country, also. If a country is moving toward the most important twin values of equalitarianism and achievement, for example, what implications does that have for competitive sport in that political entity under consideration? The following are some questions that should be asked before a strong continuing commitment is made to sponsor such involvement through governmental and/or private funding:

1. Can it be shown that involvement in competitive sport at one or the other of the three levels (i.e., amateur, semi-professional, professional) brings about desirable social values (i.e., more value than disvalue)?

2. Can it be shown that involvement in competitive sport at one or the other of the three levels (i.e., amateur, semiprofessional, or professional) brings about desirable individual values of both an intrinsic and extrinsic nature (i.e., creates more value than disvalue)?

3. If the answer to Questions #1 and #2 immediately are both affirmative (i.e., that involvement in competitive sport at any or all of the three levels postulated [i.e., amateur, semi-professional, and professional sport] provides a sufficient amount of social and individual value to warrant such promotion),can sufficient funds be made available to support or permit this promotion at any or all of the three levels listed?

4. If funding to support participation in competitive sport at any or all of the three levels (amateur, semiprofessional, professional) is not available (or such participation is not deemed advisable), should priorities--as determined by the expressed will of the people--be established about the importance of each level to the country based on careful analysis of the potential social and individual values that may accrue to the society and its citizens from such competitive sport participation at one or more levels?

Further, as one aging person who encountered corruption and sleaze in the intercollegiate athletic structure of several major universities in the United States, I retreated to a Canadian university where the term "scholar-athlete" still implies typically what it says. However, I now see problems developing on the Canadian inter-university sport scene as well. We have two choices before us. One choice is to do nothing about the "creeping semi–professionalism" that is occurring. This would require no great effort, of course. We can simply go along with the prevailing ethos of a North American society that is using sport to help in the promotion of social, as opposed to moral, character traits. In the process, "business as usual" will be supported one way or the other. A postmodern approach, conversely, would be one where specific geographic regions in Canada (the east, the far west.

Quebec, and the mid–west) reverse the trend toward semi–professionalism that is steadily developing. The pressures on university presidents and governing boards will increase steadily. Will they have wisdom and acumen to ward off this insidious possibility?

You can readily see where I am coming from with this discussion. I recommend strongly that we take a good look at what is implied when we challenge ourselves to consider what the deliberate creation of a postmodern world might do for an increasingly multiethnic Canada. Despite the change to a Conservative majority government, expanding the elements of postmodernism in Canada has a fighting chance to succeed. It would be a much better prospect for success with the New Democratic Party. In the United States–forget it! Nevertheless, in its solid effort to become a unique, multicultural society, Canada may already be implementing what may be considered some of the better aspects of the concept of "postmodernism." For better or worse–and it may well be the latter–we are not so close to "the behemoth to the South" that we can't read the handwriting on the wall about what's happening "down there."

Can We Strengthen the Postmodern Influence?

My review of selected world, European, North American, regional, and local developments occurring in the final quarter of the 20th century may have created both positive and negative thoughts on your part. You might ask how this broadly based discussion relates to a plea for consideration of an increasingly postmodern social philosophy. My response to this question is "vigorous". "It doesn't" and yet "It does." It doesn't relate or "compute" to the large majority of those functioning in the starkly modern "North American" world. The affirmative answer–that it does!–is correct if we listen to the voices of those in the substantive minority who are becoming increasingly restless with the obvious negatives of the modernism that has spread so rapidly in the modern world.

To help reverse this disturbing development, some wise scholars have recommended that the discipline of philosophy should have some connection to the world as it was described above. The late philosopher, Richard Rorty (1997), termed a so-called Neo-pragmatist, exhorted the "doomed liberal Left" in North America to join the fray again. Their presumed shame should not be bolstered by a mistaken belief that only those who agree with the Marxist position that capitalism must be eradicated are "true Lefts." Rorty recommended that philosophy once again become characterized as a "search for wisdom," a search that seeks conscientiously and capably to answer the many pressing issues and problems looming before humankind worldwide.

While most philosophers were "elsewhere engaged," some within the fold considered what has been called postmodernism carefully. For example, in *Crossing the postmodern divide* by Albert Borgmann (Chicago: The University of Chicago Press, 1992), it was refreshing to find such a clear assessment of the present situation. Time and again in discussions about postmodernism, I have encountered what I soon began to characterize as gobbledygook (i.e., planned obfuscation?). This effort by Borgmann was solid, down-to-earth, and comprehensible. However, in the final two pages, he veered to a Roman-Catholic position that he calls postmodern realism as the answer to the plight caused by modernism. It is his right, of course, to state his personal opinion after describing the current political and social situation so accurately. However, if he could have brought himself to it—if he had thought it possible for him to do so—it would have been better if he had spelled out several alternative directions for humankind to go in the 21st century. (Maybe we should be thankful that he thought any one might be able to save it!)

With his argument that "postmodernism must become, for better or worse, something other than modernism," Borgmann explains that:

> [postmodernism] already exhibits two distinct tendencies: The first is to refine technology. Here postmodernism shares with modernists an unreserved allegiance to technology, but it differs from modernism in giving technology a hyper-fine and hyper-complex design. This tendency I call hyper-modernism. The alternative tendency is to outgrow technology as a way of life and to put it to the service of reality, of the things that command our respect and grace our life. This I call postmodern realism (p. 82).

At what point could we argue that the modern epoch or era has come to an end and that civilization is ready to put hyper-modernism aside and embrace Borgmann's postmodern realism—or any form of postmodernism for that matter? Can we hope to find agreement that this epoch is approaching closure because a substantive minority of the populace is challenging many of the fundamental beliefs of modernism? The "substantive minority" may not be large enough yet, but the reader may be ready to agree that indeed the world is moving into a new epoch as the proponents of postmodernism have been affirming over recent decades. Within such a milieu all professions would probably find great difficulty crossing this so-called, postmodern gap (chasm, divide, whatever you may wish to call it). Scholars argue convincingly that many in democracies, under girded by the various rights being propounded (e.g., individual freedom, privacy), have not yet come to believe that they have found a supportive "liberal consensus" within their respective societies.

My contention is that "post-modernists"—whether they recognize themselves as belonging to this group—now form a substantive minority that supports a more humanistic, pragmatic, liberal consensus in society. Yet they recognize that present-day society is going to have difficulty crossing any such postmodern divide. Many traditionalists in democratically oriented political systems may not like everything they see in front of them today, but as they look elsewhere they flinch even more. After reviewing where society has been, and where it is now, two more questions need to be answered. Where is society heading, and—most importantly—where should it be heading?

As despairing as one might be of society's direction today, the phenomenon of postmodernism—with its accompanying deconstructionist analytic technique affirming the idea that the universe is valueless with no absolute—brings one up short quickly. Take your choice: bleak pessimism or blind optimism. The former seems to be more dangerous to humankind's future that that of an idealistic future "under the sheltering arms of a Divine Father." Yet, some argue that Nietzsche's philosophy of being, knowledge, and morality supports the basic dichotomy espoused by the philosophy of being in the post-modernistic position. I can understand at once, therefore, why it meets with opposition by those whose thought has been supported by traditional theocentrism.

A better approach, I recommend, might be one of "positive meliorism" in which humankind is exhorted to "take it from here and do its best to improve the world situation." In the process we should necessarily inquire: "What happened to the "Enlightenment ideal"? This was supposed to be America's chief criterion of progress, but it has gradually but steadily undergone such a decisive change since the founding of the Republic. That change is at once a cause and a reflection of our current disenchantment with technology.

Post-modernists do indeed subscribe to a humanistic, anthropocentric belief as opposed to the traditional theocentric position. They would probably subscribe, therefore to what Berelson and Steiner in the mid-1960s postulated as a behavioral science image of man and woman (1964). This view characterized the human as a creature continuously adapting reality to his or her own ends. Such thought undoubtedly challenges the authority of theological positions, dogmas, ideologies, and some scientific "infallibles".

A moderate post-modernist—holding a position I feel able to subscribe to if I were able to bring it all into focus—would at least listen to what the "authority" had written or said before criticizing or rejecting it. A fully committed post-modernist goes his or her own way by early, almost automatic, rejection of all tradition. Then this person presumably relies simply on a personal interpretation and subsequent diagnosis to muster the authority to challenge any or all icons or "lesser gods" extant in society.

Concluding Statement

In conclusion, I have argued that a *moderate* post-modernist would feel most comfortable seeking to achieve his or her personal, professional, and social/environmental goals through the stance that has been described in this monograph. This position would be directly opposed to the traditional stifling position of, for example, "essentialist" theological realists or idealists. The world is in the process of changing. It *has* changed significantly! Conflicting "world religions" and arbitrary political ideologies are getting in the way of civilization's progress. The conflicts they cause may well destroy humankind. A more pragmatic "value-is-that-which-is proven-through-experience" orientation that could emerge as one legacy of postmodernism would leave the future open-ended. That is the way it ought to be for the future on this "speck" in the infinite universe (multi-verse?) that we call "Earth."

References

Aburdene, P. & Naisbitt, J. (1992). *Megatrends for women*. NY: Villard Books. 388 p.

Anderson, W.T. (1997). *The future of the self: Inventing the postmodern person.* NY: Tarcher/Putnam.

Berelson, B. and Steiner, G. A. (1964). *Human behavior*. NY: Harcourt, Brace, Jovanovich.

Berman, M. (2001) *The twilight of American culture*. NY: W.W. Norton.

Bogle. J. (2007). The battle for the soul of capitalism. NY: Viking.

Borgman, A. (1993) *Crossing the postmodern divide*. Chicago: The University of Chicago Press.

Commager, H. S. (1961). A quarter century--Its advances. *Look*, 25, 10 (June 6), 80-91.

Friedman, T. L. (2005) A brief history of the 21st century. NY: Farrar, Straus, and Giroux

Huntington, S. P. (1998). *The clash of civilizations (and the remaking of world order)*. NY: Touchstone.

Lipset. S. M. (1973). National character. In D. Koulack & D. Perlman (Eds.), *Readings in social psychology: Focus on Canada*. Toronto: Wiley.

Marx, L. (1990). Does improved technology mean progress? In A.H. Teich (Ed.)*Technology and the Future* (5th Ed.) (pp. 5-9). NY: St. Martin's.

Naisbitt, J. (1982). *Megatrends*. New York: Warner.\

Naisbitt, J. & Aburdene, P. (1990). *Megatrends* 2000. New York: Wm. Morrow.

Rees-Mogg, W. (1988). The decline of the Olympics into physical and moral squalor. *Coaching Focus*, 8 (1988),

Rorty, R. (1997) *Achieving our country*. Cambridge, MA: Harvard University Press

Ten events that shook the world between 1984 and 1994. (Special Report). *Utne Reader*, 62 (March/April 1994): 58-74

Toynbee, A. J. (1947). *A study of history*. NY: Oxford University Press.

Selection 10
Several Final "Nonagenarian Natterings"

I am finding that it's somewhat easier to get older than it is to get wiser. The pace of life seems to be increasing, also. However, it's not the pace of life that worries me; it's just that upcoming sudden stop at the end…

However, I do want to pontificate a moment on what I consider to be the two burning issues related to my professional pursuits over the past 68 years. I am greatly concerned about the fact that the large majority of "normal" and "special needs" children and youth are not getting a quality physical activity education program that would help them live life more fully in the future–and actually help them live longer as well.

Further, and this factor has a direct relationship to my first issue, I do strongly believe that competitive sport may gradually be doing more harm to the world than good! Somehow, the more sport is professionalized as a result of globalism, capitalism, and technology, the more its potential beneficial impact on society declines.

Sport has become a reflection of a society that has been influenced unfavorably by these developments. The ideals of honesty, sportsmanship, good will, and fair play are threatened daily.

I must bring this volume to a close. My friends, I must tell you that I'll try hard to keep up my enthusiasm for "the 90s decade" I'm 92 today, as I write these words, and I doubt if I'll make to the elusive 100 number. It becoming increasingly difficult. The other day I was sitting in a rocking chair, and I had to ask Anne to help me get it going… I think I know all the answers. But nobody wants to ask me any questions any more…!

Finally, I leave you with those immortal words by that famous 18th-19th century German literary figure, Johann Wolfgang von Goethe. "Es irrt den Mensch solang er strebt."

No one ever figured out what he meant with that thought. No, seriously, these stirring words drilled into me by my favorite German professor, were translated as "The human errs, but strive he must." I have "erred", and I have "striven".

Satchell Page, the legendary Black baseball pitcher caught the spirit of Goethe's exhortation, in these more understandable words:

"DON'T LOOK BACK--AND DON'T REST ON YOUR OARS-- THEY'RE GAINING ON YOU!

Finally, we look forward to an uncertain future. The world has many problems, and we **OURSELVES** (!) must solve them if this "noble experiment" is to succeed.

The odds don't look good. We can only hope that humans of intelligence and good will can make it all work…

You folks "out there" have to "take it from here". I wish you well…

Appendix A
Philosophic Self-Evaluation in Life and Education

What follows is the latest version of a philosophic, self-evaluation checklist designed for men and women who are specializing in the profession of education. I developed this checklist originally in the early 1950s, but it has been revised and updated regularly over the years to reflect all of the positions, tendencies, and stances described below. By employing this instructional device carefully and honestly–while appreciating the subjectivity of an instrument such as this–aspiring professionals in education will be able to determine quite accurately their philosophy of life (including an ethical position) and their philosophy of education. (Additional subsections not included here have been developed for the fields of health & safety education, physical activity education, and recreation as well.)

Before examining himself or herself, we suggest that each person study briefly the Freedom-Constraint Spectrum below. (You will be asked to do this again after you have completed the checklist and have evaluated your personal position.) *Keep in mind that the primary criterion on which this is based is the concept of 'personal freedom' in contrast to 'personal constraint'. Herbert J. Muller's definition of freedom (1954) calls it "the condition of being able to choose and to carry out purposes" in one's personal living pattern.*

Within our social environment, the words "progressive" or "liberal" and "conservative" or "traditional" have historically related to policies favoring individual freedom and policies favoring adherence to tradition, respectively. For this reason, the more traditional positions or stances are shown to the right on the spectrum, and the more progressive ones are shown to the left. The analytic approach to doing philosophy is included in the checklist, but it is not shown on the spectrum because it has indeed become "philosophy in a new key." The earlier, mainstream positions in educational philosophy are indicated in parentheses on the figure below. Other pertinent definitions of positions on the freedom-constraint spectrum are offered immediately below the figure itself.

Figure 1
The Freedom-Constraint Spectrum

Eclecticism*

Existentialism**　　　　Traditional
(atheistic, agnostic,　　or　(Idealism)
or theistic)

Somewhat Progressive　　　　Traditional
(Reconstructionism)　　　(Naturalistic Realism)

Progressive　　　　　　　Traditional
(Pragmatic Naturalism)　　(Rational Humanism)

Strongly Progressive　　　　Strongly Traditional
(Romantic Naturalism)　　　(Scholastic Realism)

ANARCHY　　　　　　　　　　DICTATORSHIP

"the left"　　　　　　　　　　　"the right"

Analytic--a philosophic outlook, actually with ancient origins, that moved ahead strongly in the twentieth century. The assumption here has been that our ordinary language has many defects that need to be corrected. There is concern also with conceptual analysis. Another objective is "the rational reconstruction of the language of science" (Abraham Kaplan). Basically, the preoccupation is with analysis as opposed to philosophical system-building.

* The so-called eclectic approach is placed in the center because it assumes that the person evaluating himself or herself has selected several positions on opposite sides of the spectrum. Most would argue that eclecticism is philosophically indefensible, while some believe that "patterned eclecticism" (or "reasoned incoherence" as this position has been called) represents a stance which most of us hold.

** Existentialistic--a permeating influence rather than a full-blown philosophical position. Keep in mind that there are those with either an atheistic, agnostic, or theistic orientation. This position has been shown slightly to the left of center because within this stance(tendency) there is a strong emphasis on individual freedom of choice.

WHAT DO I BELIEVE?
(A professional, self-evaluation checklist)

<u>Instructions:</u> Read the statements below carefully, section by section, and indicate by an X the statement in each section that seems closest to your own personal belief.

Check your answers only after all FIVE sections have been completed. Then complete the summarizing tally on the answer page. Take note of apparent inconsistencies in your overall position. Finally, return to the freedom-constraint spectrum above to discover your "location" whether in the center--or to the right or left.

> Note: Many of the words, terms, phrases, etc. have been obtained from the work of philosophers, educational philosophers, and sport and physical education philosophers, living or deceased. I am most grateful for this assistance, but in the final analysis decided to leave them unidentified so as not to prejudice the person taking the test. In this self-evaluation check list, sections relating to the allied professions (e.g., recreation) have been deliberately omitted, but they are available upon request.

Keep in mind that we are not seeking to make the case that, for example, a position taken under (say) Category I will result by logical deduction in a comparable position being taken in a following category either within the education or sport and physical education categories. Nevertheless, positions taken in these latter categories should, to be consistent, probably be grounded on philosophical presuppositions stated earlier.

Category I
THE NATURE OF REALITY (METAPHYSICS)

A. _____ Experience and nature constitute both the form and also the content of the entire universe. There is no such thing as a pre-established order of affairs in the world. Reality is evolving, and humanity appears to be a most important manifestation of the natural process. The impact of cultural forces upon people is fundamental, and every effort should be made to understand them as we strive to build the best type of a group-centered culture. In other words, the structure of cultural reality should be our foremost concern. Cultural determinants have shaped human history, and a crucial stage has now been reached in the development of life on the planet. Our efforts must now be focused on the building of a world culture.

B. _____ I believe that the metaphysical and normative types of philosophizing have lost their basis for justification in the twentieth century. Their presumed wisdom has not been able to withstand the rigor of careful analysis. Sound theory is available to humankind through the application of scientific method to problem-solving. So what is the exact nature of philosophy? Who is in a position to answer the ultimate questions about the nature of reality? The scientist is, of course, and the philosopher must become the servant of science through conceptual analysis and the rational reconstruction of language. Accordingly the philosopher must resign himself or herself to dealing with important, but lesser, questions than the origin of the universe and the nature of the human being--and what implications this might have for everyday conduct.

C. _____ The world of men and women is a human one, and it is from the contest of this human world that all the abstractions of science derive their meaning ultimately. There is the world of material objects, of course, that extends in mathematical space with only quantitative and measurable properties, but we humans are first and foremost "concrete involvements" within the world. Existence precedes essence, and it is up to men and women to decide their own fate. This presumably makes the human different from all other creatures on earth. It appears true that people can actually transform life's present condition, and thus the future may well stand open to these unusual beings.

D. _____ Nature is an emergent evolution, and the human's frame of reality is limited to nature as it functions. The world is characterized by activity and

161

change. Rational man and woman have developed through organic evolution over millions of years, and the world is yet incomplete--a reality that is constantly undergoing change because of a theory of emergent novelty that appears to be operating within the universe. People enjoy true freedom of will. This freedom is achieved through continuous and developmental learning from experience.

E. _____ Mind as experience by all people is basic and real. The entire universe is mind essentially. The human is more than just a body; people possess souls, and such possession makes them of a higher order than all other creatures on earth. The order of the world is due to the manifestation in space and time of an eternal and spiritual reality. The individual is simply part of the whole. It is therefore a person's duty to learn as much about the Absolute as possible. Within this position there is divided opinion regarding the problem of monism or pluralism (one force or more than one force). The individual person has freedom to determine which way he or she will go in life. The individual can relate to the moral law in the universe, or else he or she can turn against it.

Category II
ETHICS AND MORALITY (Axiology/Values)

A. _____ The source of all human experience lies in the regularities of the universe. Things don't just happen; they happen because many interrelated forces make them occur in a particular way. Humans in this environment are confronted by one reality only--that which we perceive is it! The "life of reason" is extremely important, a position that emanates originally from Aristotle who placed intellectual virtues above moral virtues in his hierarchy. Many holding this stance believe that all elements of nature, including people, are inextricably linked together in an endless chain of causes and effects. Thus, they accept a sort of ethical determinism--i.e., what people are morally is determined by response patterns imprinted in their being by both heredity and environment. A large number in the world carry this fundamental position still further by adding a theological component; for them the highest good is ultimate union with God, the Creator, who is responsible for teleological and supernatural reality. As a creature of God, human goodness is reached by the spirituality of the form attained as the individual achieves emancipation from the material (or the corporeal). The belief is that a person's being contains potential energy that may be guided or directed toward God or away from Him; thus, what the individual does in the final analysis determines whether such action will be regarded as right or wrong.

B. _____ There should be no distinction between moral goods and natural goods. There has been a facts/values dualism in existence, and this should be eradicated as soon as possible by the use of scientific method applied to ethical situations. Thus, we should employ reflective thinking to obtain the ideas that will function as tentative solutions for the solving of life's concrete problems. Those ideas can serve as hypotheses to be tested in life experimentally. If the ideas work in solving problematic situations, they become true. In this way we have empirical verification of hypotheses tending to bring theory and practice into a closer union. When we achieve agreement in factual belief, agreement in attitudes about this subject should soon follow. In this way science can ultimately bring about complete agreement on factual belief or knowledge about human behavior. Thus there will be a continuous adaptation of values to the culture's changing needs that will in turn effect the directed reconstruction of all social institutions.

C. _____ The problems of ethics should be resolved quite differently than they have throughout most of history. Ethics cannot be resolved completely through the application of scientific method, although an ethical dispute must be on a factual level--i.e., factual statements must be distinguished from value statements. Ethics should be normative in the sense that we have moral standards. However, this is a difficult task because the term "good" appears to be indefinable. The terms used to define or explain ethical standards or norms should be analyzed logically in a careful manner. Social scientists should be enlisted to help in the determination of the validity of factual statements, as well as in the analysis of conflicting attitudes as progress is determined. Ethical dilemmas in modern life can be resolved through the combined efforts of the philosophical moralist and the scientist. The resultant beliefs may in time change people's attitudes. Basically, the task is to establish a hierarchy of reasons with a moral basis.

D. _____ Good and bad, and rightness and wrongness, are relative and vary according to the situation or culture involved (i.e., the needs of a situation are there and then in that society or culture). Each ethical decision is highly individual, initially at least, since every situation has its particularity. The free, authentic individual decides to accept responsibility when he or she responds to a human situation and seeks to answer the need of an animal, person, or group. How does the "witness react to the world?" Guidance in the making of an ethical decision may come either from "outside," from intuition, from one's own conscience, from reason, from empirical investigation, etc. Thus it can be argued that there are no absolutely valid ethical principles or universal laws.

E. _____ Ethics and morality are based on cosmic laws, and we are good if we figure out how to share actively in them. If we have problems of moral conduct, we have merely to turn to the Lord's commandments for solutions to all moral problems. Yet there is nothing deterministic here, because the individual himself or herself has an active role to play in determining which ethical actions will bring him or her into closer unity with the supreme Self. However, the fact of the matter is that God is both the source and the goal of the values for which we strive in our everyday lives. In this approach the presence of evil in the world is recognized as a real human experience to be met and conquered. The additional emphasis here is on logical argument to counter the ever-present threat of the philosophy of science. This is countered by the argument that there is unassailable moral law inherent in the Universe that presents people with obligations to duty (e.g., honesty is a good that is universal).

F. _____ Our social environment is inextricably related to the many struggles of peoples for improvement of the quality of life--how to place more good in our lives than bad, so to speak. We are opposed to any theory that delineates values as absolute and separates them from everyday striving within a social milieu. Actually the truth of values can be determined by established principles of evidence. In an effort to achieve worldwide consensus on any and all values, our stated positions on issues and controversial matters must necessarily be criticized in public forums. Cultural realities that affect values should be re-oriented through the achievement of agreed-upon purposes (i.e., through social consensus and social-self-realization on a worldwide basis). The goal, then, is to move toward a comprehensive pattern of values that provides both flexibility and variety. This should be accompanied by sufficient freedom to allow the individual to achieve individual and social values in his or her life. However, we must not forget that the majority does rule in evolving democracies, and at times wrong decisions are made. Keeping in mind that the concept of 'democracy' will prevail only to the extent that "enlightened" decisions are made, we must guarantee the ever-present role of the critical minority as it seeks to alter any consensus established. A myth of utopian vision should guide our efforts as we strive toward the achievement of truly human ethical values in the life experiences of all our citizens.

Category III
EDUCATIONAL AIMS AND OBJECTIVES

A. _____ Socialization of the child has become equally as important as his or her intellectual development as a key educational aim in this century. There should be concern, however, because many educational philosophers seem to assume the position that children are to be fashioned so that they will conform to a prior notion of what they should be. Even the progressivists seem to have failed in their effort to help the learner "posture himself or herself." If it does become possible to get general agreement on a set of fundamental dispositions to be formed, should the criterion employed for such evaluation be a public one (rather than personal and private)? Education should seek to "awaken awareness" in the learner--awareness of the person as a single subjectivity in the world. Increased emphasis is needed on the arts and social sciences, and the student should freely and creatively choose his or her own pattern of education.

B. _____ Social-self-realization is the supreme value in education. The realization of this ideal is most important for the individual in the social setting--a world culture. Positive ideals should be molded toward the evolving democratic ideal by a general education which is group-centered and in which the majority determines the acceptable goals. However, once that majority opinion is determined, all are obligated to conform until such majority opinion can be reversed (the doctrine of "defensible partiality"). Nevertheless, education by means of "hidden coercion" is to be scrupulously avoided. Learning itself is explained by the organismic principle of functional psychology. Social intelligence acquired teaches people to control and direct their urges as they concur with or attempt to modify cultural purposes.

C. _____ The concept of 'education' has become much more complex that was ever realized before. Because of the various meanings of the term "education," talking about educational aims and objectives is almost a hopeless task unless a myriad of qualifications is used for clarification. The term ("education") has now become what is called a "family-resemblance" term in philosophy. Thus we need to qualify our meaning to explain to the listener whether we mean (1) the subject-matter; (2) the activity of education carried on by teachers; (3) the process of being educated (or learning) that is occurring; (4) the result, actual or intended, or No.2 and No.3 Immediately above taking place through the employment of that which comprises No.1 above; (5) the discipline, or field of enquiry and investigation; and (6) the profession whose members are involved professionally with all of the aspects of education described above. With this understanding, it is then possible to make some determination about which specific objectives the profession of education should strive for as it moves in the direction of the achievement of long range aims.

D. _____ The general aim of education is more education. Education in the broadest sense can be nothing else than the changes made in human beings by their experience. Participation by students in the formation of aims and objectives is absolutely essential to generate the all-important desired interest required for the finest educational process to occur. Social efficiency (i.e., societal socialization) can well be considered the general aim of education. Pupil growth is a paramount goal. This means that the individual is placed at the center of the educational experience.

E. _____ A philosophy which holds that the aim of education is the acquisition of verified knowledge of the environment; which recognizes the value of content as well as the activities involved; and which takes into account the external determinants of human behavior. Education is the acquisition of the art of the utilization of knowledge. The primary task of education is to transmit knowledge, knowledge without which civilization could not continue to flourish. Whatever people have discovered to be true because it conforms to reality should be handed down to future generations as the social or cultural tradition. Some holding this philosophy believe that the good life emanates from cooperation with God's grace, and believe further that the development of the Christian virtues is obviously of greater worth than learning or anything else.

F. _____ Through education the developing organism becomes what it latently is. All education may be said to have a religious significance, the meaning of which is that there is a "moral imperative" on education. As the person's mind strives to realize itself, there is the possibility of the Absolute within the individual mind. Education should aid the child to adjust to the basic realities (the spiritual ideals of truth, beauty, and goodness) that the history of the race has furnished us. The basic values of human living are health, character, social justice, skill, art, love, knowledge, philosophy, and religion.

Category IV
THE EDUCATIVE PROCESS
(Epistemology)

A. _____ Understanding the nature of knowledge will clarify the nature of reality. Nature is the medium by which the Absolute communicates to us. Basically, knowledge comes only from the mind, a mind which must offer and receive ideas. Mind and matter are qualitatively different. A finite mind emanates through heredity from another finite mind. Thought is the standard by which all else in the world is judged. An individual attains truth for himself or herself by examining the wisdom of the past through his or her own mind. Reality, viewed in this way, is a system of logic and order that has been established by the Universal Mind. Experimental testing helps to determine what the truth really is.

B. _____ The child experiences an "awareness of being" in his/her subjective life about the time of puberty--and is never the same thereafter. The young person truly becomes aware of his or her own existence, and the fact that there is now a responsibility for one's own conduct. After this point in life, education must be an "act of discovery" to be truly effective. Somehow the teacher should help the young person to become involved personally with his or her education, and also with the world situation in which such an education is taking place. Objective or subjective knowledge should be personally selected and 'appropriated" by the youth unto himself or herself, or else it will be relatively meaningless in that particular life. Thus it matters not whether logic, scientific evidence, sense perception, intuition, or revelation is claimed as the basis of knowledge acquisition, no learning will take place for that individual self until the child or young person decides that such learning is "true" for him or her in that person's life. Therefore the young person knows when he or she knows!

C. _____ Knowledge is the result of a process of thought with a useful purpose. Truth is not only to be tested by its correspondence with reality, but also by its practical results. Knowledge is earned through experience and is an instrument of verification. Mind has evolved in the natural order as a more flexible means whereby people adapt themselves to the world. Learning takes place when interest and effort unite to produce the desired result. A psychological order of learning (problem-solving as explained through scientific method) is ultimately more useful (productive?) than a logical arrangement (proceeding from the simple fact to the complex conclusion). However, we shouldn't forget that there is always a social context to learning, and the curriculum itself should be adapted to the particular society for which it is intended.

D. _____ Concern with the educative process should begin with an understanding of the terms that are typically employed for discussion purposes within any educational program. The basic assumption is that these terms are usually employed loosely and often improperly. For example, to be precise we should be explaining that a student is offered educational experiences in a classroom and/or laboratory setting. Through the employment of various types and techniques of instructional methodology (e.g., lectures), he or she hears facts, increases the scope of information and/or knowledge, and learns to comprehend and interpret the material (understanding). Possessing various kinds and amounts of ability or aptitude, students   gradually develop competencies and a certain degree or level of skill. It is hoped that certain appreciations about the worth of the individual student's experiences will be developed, and that he or she will form certain attitudes about familial, societal, and professional life that lie ahead. Finally, societal values and norms, along with other social influences, will help educators, fulfilling role within their collectivities and subcollectivities, determine the best methods (with accompanying experimentation, of course) of achieving socially acceptable educational goals.

E. _____ An organismic approach to the learning process is basic. Thought cannot be independent of certain aspects of the organism. This is because thought is related integrally with emotional and muscular functions. The person's mind enables him or her to cope with the problems of human life in a social environment within a physical world. Social intelligence is actually closely related to scientific method. Certain operational concepts, inseparable from metaphysics and axiology (beliefs about reality and values), focus on the reflective thought, problem-solving, and social consensus necessary for the gradual transformation of the culture.

F. _____ There are two major learning (epistemological) theories of knowledge in this philosophical stance. One states that the aim of knowledge is to bring into awareness the object as it really is. The other emphasizes that objects are "represented" in the human's consciousness, not "presented." Students should develop habits and skills involved with acquiring knowledge, with using knowledge practically to meet life's problems, and with realizing the enjoyment that life offers. A second variation of learning theory (epistemological belief) here indicates that the child develops his or her intellect by employing reason to learn a subject. The principal educational aims proceeding hand in hand with learning theory here would be the same for all people at all times in all places. Others with a more religious orientation holding this position, basically add to this stance that education is the process by which people seek to link themselves ultimate with their Creator.

Answers: Read only after all five questions have been completed. Record your answer to each part of the checklist on the summarizing tally form below.

I. The Nature of Reality (Metaphysics)

a. Somewhat Progressive (Reconstructionism, Brameld)
b. Analytic (Analytic Philosophy)
c. Existentialistic (atheistic, agnostic, or theistic)
d. Progressive (Pragmatic Naturalism; Ethical Naturalism)
e. Traditional (Philosophic Idealism)
f. Traditional (Philosophic Realism, with elements of Naturalistic Realism, Rational Humanism, and positions within Catholic educational philosophy)

II. Ethics (Axiology)

a. Traditional (including elements of Strongly Traditional; Philosophic Realism, plus theology)
b. Progressive (Pragmatic Naturalism; Ethical Naturalism)
c. Analytic (Emotive Theory; "Good Reasons" Approach)
d. Existentialistic (atheistic, agnostic, and some Christians)
e. Traditional (Philosophic Idealism; Protestant Christian)
f. Somewhat Progressive (Reconstructionism, Brameld; Ethical Naturalism)

III. Educational Aims and Objectives

a. Existentialistic
b. Somewhat Progressive

    c. Analytic

    d. Progressive

    e. Traditional (including elements of Strongly Traditional)

    f. Traditional

IV. The Educative Process (Epistemology)

    a. Traditional

    b. Existentialistic

    c. Progressive

    d. Analytic

    e. Somewhat Progressive

    f. Traditional (including elements of Strongly Traditional)

Table 1

Summarizing Tally For Self-Evaluation

Note: For explanation of symbols, please see key below.

	Prg.	Prg-S.	Exist.	Trd.	Trd-S.	Anal.
Category I Metaphysics	_____	_____	_____	_____	_____	_____
Category II Ethics & Morality	_____	_____	_____	_____	_____	_____
Category III Educational Objectives	_____	_____	_____	_____	_____	_____
Category IV Epistemology	_____	_____	_____	_____	_____	_____
Totals	_____	_____	_____	_____	_____	_____

Key: Prg. = progressive; Prg.-S. = somewhat progressive; Exist.=existentialistic; Trd. = traditional; Trd-S = strongly traditional; Anal. = analytic

Further Instructions: It should now be possible--keeping in mind the subjectivity of an instrument such as this--to determine your position approximately based on the answers that you have given and then tallied on the form immediately above.

At the very least you should be able to tell if you are progressive, traditional, existentialistic, or analytic in your philosophic approach.

If you discover considerable eclecticism in your overall position or stance--that is, checks that place you on opposite sides of the Freedom-Constraint Spectrum, or some vacillation with checks in the existentialistic or analytic categories--you may wish then to analyze your positions or stances more closely to see if your overall position is philosophically defensible.

Keep in mind that your choices under Category I (Metaphysics or Nature of Reality) and Category II (Axiology/Values) are basic and in all probability have a strong influence on your subsequent selections.

Now please examine the Freedom-Constraint Spectrum at the beginning of this section again. Keep in mind that "Existentialistic" is not considered a position or stance as the others are (e.g., Traditional or Philosophic Idealism). Also, if you tend to be "Analytic," this means that your pre-occupation is with analysis as opposed to any philosophic/theologic system-building.

Finally, then, after tallying the answers (your "score" above), and keeping in mind that the goal is not to "pigeonhole you forever more," did this self-evaluation checklist show you to be:

( ) Strongly Progressive--4 checks left of center on the Spectrum?

( ) Progressive—2 to 3 checks left of center?

( ) Somewhat Progressive—1 to 2 checks left of center?

( ) Eclectic--checks in 2 or 3 positions on both the right and left of the Spectrum's center?

( ) Somewhat Traditional—1 to 2 checks right of center?

( ) Traditional—2 to 3 checks right of center?

( ) Strongly Traditional—3 or 4 checks right of center?

( ) Existentialistic—3 to 4 checks (including Category I) relating to this stance?

( ) Analytic—3 to 4 checks (including Category I) relating to this approach to doing philosophy?

Appendix B
Where Are You On a Socio-Political Spectrum?
(A Self-Evaluation Questionnaire for North Americans)

Instructions:

What really is *your* socio-political stance or position? This questionnaire will help you figure out where you really stand--not where you may nominally think that you are. When someone asks, "Are you a conservative or a liberal (or progressive)? What do you say in response? How can you justify such an answer?

> *(Note: Keep in mind that these responses do not necessarily equate with the presently stated platforms of existing political parties in either the United States or Canada.)*

Very few people will admit that they are radical or reactionary (i.e., far left or far right). Even if you are neutral, or middle-of-the-road, it should be possible to make that determination. Why is this important? Simply because those with an "ordered mind" ought to be able to state their beliefs and opinions with reasonable consistency throughout based on a set of comprehensible values.

Answer the following questions to the best of your ability in accordance with your reason and/or conscience. You are *designating how you want it to be*! Where possible, a position has been carefully worded to represent one of the following six positions: (1) **Reactionary**, (2) **Conservative,** (3) **Moderate Conservative**, (4) **Moderate Liberal**, (5) **Liberal**, AND (6) **Radical**. In some instances, allowing only two options for response (i.e., agreement or disagreement) was deemed best.

Please encircle the letter (a, b, etc.) that appears before the answer you select. On any given issue, a middle-of-the-road position to the right or left on a spectrum would fluctuate between +3 and +1 or between -3 and -1. When you are finished with the self-evaluation, and the scores are totaled, it should be possible for you to designate yourself one way or the other. However, you may be an *eclectic* (i.e., a person with widely distributed responses from both sides of the spectrum). Perhaps you will be a truly *middle-of-the-road person* (i.e., generally neutral on most questions).

The scoring system is included at the end of the

questionnaire. In each question, please select the answer that comes the closest to reflecting *how you would like it to be* (!)

==

Figure 1
Where Do You Fall on the Socio-Political Spectrum?

Eclecticism*
(Maverick*)
(-6 to +6**)

Moderate	Moderate
Liberal	Conservative
(-7 to -19)	(+7 to +19)

Liberal   Conservative
(-20 to -32)   (+20 to +32)

Radical   Reactionary
(-33 to -45)   (+33 to +45)

"the left"   "the right"

* The so-called eclectic or "maverick" approach is placed in the center because it assumes that the person evaluating himself or herself has selected several positions on *opposite* sides of the spectrum. Most would argue that eclecticism--or a position that might be called "maverick"--is philosophically indefensible. Because of the subjectivity involved, some believe that "patterned eclecticism" (or "reasoned incoherence") represents a stance which most of us hold.

** The numerals refer to scores made on the spectrum scale.

==

Question #1: THE UNITED NATIONS.

The place of the United Nations in world government should be:

a. **Negligible**--(i.e., advisory only or possibly eliminated).

b. **Minor**--and used for voluntary arbitration of international disputes only.

c. **As at present**--with members of Council having veto power.

d. **Enlarged somewhat** --and characterized by more adequate enforcement of decisions.

e. **Expanded somewhat**--and involved with actual enforcement of peacekeeping.

f. **Expanded greatly**--and hold the leading position in world government (a similar relationship as a federal government does to its states or provinces.

Question #2: FOREIGN AID.

North Americans should:

a. Stop all foreign aid except when serious natural disasters occur.

b. Help friendly nations and/or neutral nations strengthen themselves against communistic and similar undemocratic nations by providing economic and educational assistance.

c. Provide aid to developing nations to the best of our ability, but only to those who ask for such aid and are willing to use it for sound economic development. The channeling of aid through an international agency is basic.

d. Keep foreign aid to a minimum, getting involved only when it is clearly in our self-interest.

e. Provide assistance to free and/or neutral nations only.

f.   Aid economically any needy country that requests such help for basic services.

Question #3: WAR AND PEACE.

As to military affairs and defense, North Americans should:

a.   Work to outlaw war through unilateral disarmament by *all* nations.

b.   Intervene militarily only when required (by United Nations and NATO) when the need is extreme--and then only in an effort to bring peace and to protect further loss of life. Major powers should disarm to an "irreducible minimum."

c.   Give military assistance to free or neutral nations when they request it. Encourage the idea of disarmament.

d.   Help friendly and/or neutral nations with military assistance against infiltration by undemocratic ideologies (e.g., communism).

e.   Stand prepared to protect the free world and "third– world" nations with military forces at all times.

f.   Deal ruthlessly with naked aggression wherever it occurs (including use of nuclear power).

Question #4: HOSTAGE CRISES.

In a hostage crisis where one country holds North American citizens at ransom (or for whatever purpose) warrants the following action:

a.   An urgent request for an explanation, assurance of safe release, and reparation for damages at the first possible moment.

b.   Armed invasion as soon as it becomes apparent that the hostages taken are in danger and will not be released.

c.   A protest through diplomatic channels for an explanation with a plea for swift action and the safety of the hostages.

d.   An immediate warning that such kidnapping and

terrorist activity will not be tolerated. The foreign government concerned should understand that some direct action will be taken if hostages are not released by a specified date.

   e.   The immediate establishment of a naval blockade to the extent possible along with the implementation of other sanctions possible (e.g., freezing of assets).

   f.   A sharp protest through diplomatic channels indicating that consideration will be given to what measures might be taken to effect the release of the hostages.

Question #5: PROTESTS AND RIOTING.

Youth, both at home and abroad, are causing considerable concern to governmental officials at all levels. I feel that young people:

   a.   Must be made to respect law and order. Rioters who loot should be warned and then shot if they do not stop. Foreign nationals, immigrants, and other marginal persons in these groups should be rooted out, jailed, and/or deported.

   b.   Are in many cases, attempting to move positively toward an improved national and international order. They should be given many different types of roles to play, as well as opportunities to improve the situation through involvement.

   c.   Are concerned and need positive leadership from adults who have experience and expertise in such matters. Only a small percent of these activists are radical and need truly firm control.

   d.   Are justified in their struggle to change the basic nature of the society. Ethnic minority groups, Blacks (in the States), and young people should not have to wait forever for much-   needed change. Many fundamental institutions must be rebuilt from the ground up.

   e.   Are proving in many cases to be ungrateful brats. Lax, frightened adults have allowed them to get out of hand too often. Strong adult leadership is required.

f. Are troubled and need guidance from qualified personnel.
Only a relatively few are real troublemakers who need to
be curbed by force. The large majority of youth will turn out to be decent,
law-abiding adults.

Question #6: PUBLIC WELFARE.

Public welfare programs in North America are:

a. Urgently needed and should be coordinated by the federal government. There should be a guaranteed annual income for all needy families sufficient to provide a reasonable standard of living pro-rated to the cost-of-living in the geographical region involved. Billions are needed as soon as possible to upgrade all aspects of the lives of the poor and neglected members of society.

b. Best left to states and local governments to provide only the most needy with some assistance. Heads of families (or close relatives) should work to provide for the welfare of their families (and/or close relatives). Government handouts should be kept to an absolute minimum.

c. Needed on a limited basis from all levels of government, but experience has shown that the federal government should set and enforce national standards. In this way, all families will have sufficient resources to maintain at least a minimum standard of living. Current disincentives to work must somehow be removed.

d. Unfortunately necessary. Somehow the current disincentives toward work must be eliminated. All male and female recipients should be worked back into the job force--even by doing public service work for their welfare payments. Perhaps by introducing national or regional standards that take into
consideration cost of living indexes in the various "high" welfare states.

e. Positively dangerous to the future of our democratic societies on the continent because they are inexorably bringing about a decay of moral fiber. In our North American culture people work for a living. We must become firmer. If those currently on the dole get hungry enough, they will find some work to do to support themselves and their families.

f. A "sop" to mislead the poor and trick them into acceptance of the capitalist system. The nation's wealth should be redistributed so as to assure virtual equality for all people who are willing to be gainfully employed citizens. The current
systematic degradation and exploitation of the poor must stop.

Question #7: FREEDOM OF SPEECH AND PRESS.

The rights of freedom of speech and press contained, for example, in the First Amendment of the U.S. Constitution:

a. Are part of the heritage of free men and women on this continent, but subversive and immoral elements have been allowed to take advantage of these rights. Certain people and related social influences threaten to destroy the fabric of freedom.

b. Are a vital part of the America's and Canada's heritage. We all profit from new and different ideas. However, it is necessary to limit speech and action that present a "clear and present danger" to our civil and moral welfare.

c. Are perhaps the most important rights granted to citizens by government in constitutions and bills of right. Movements to dilute or "balance away" these rights in the interest of national security have typically been misdirected. Suppression of speech and movement should be carried out only in extreme situations.

d. Are a part of the democratic heritage in the United States, but freedom does not mean license to say anything one wants to say at any time. There must be strong checks on pornography or revolutionary speech and action.

e. Are a myth because the corporate, capitalistic power structure through employment of the mass media conspires to suppress free and creative speech and thought.

f. Were grossly misinterpreted by past Supreme Court judgments. All obscene and subversive materials and actions must be suppressed to protect our country from the radical revolutionary threat at home and the planned world take-over elsewhere.

Question #8: ECONOMICS & BUSINESS.
Please read the following statement carefully. Then try to categorize yourself in one of the ways indicated.

One of the first concerns of a federal government in North America should be the provision of a sound business climate. This is accomplished best if the government employs only minimum restrictions on businesses and corporations. For example, wage and hour legislation is wrong. Any contract that developed—if there must be one—should be arranged strictly between employers and employees.

Concurrently, every effort should be made to stay with a balanced budget. In fact, an economy will not really be (safe and) sound until steady, sensible fiscal policies bring about a significant reduction in a national debt. However, it is important, also, not to increase the burden on taxpayers even though a strong national defense is necessary. Big business is taxed so heavily that people's dividends on their investments are becoming unreasonably small. Inflation must stay at a reasonable level, and the economy needs ever-present stimulation.

Through reasonable policies about spending both at home and abroad, we should be able to develop a type of revenue—sharing in the years ahead. Through the stimulation of private enterprise, with occasional block grants of money with no strings attached made to states or provinces ha are hard pressed financially, we should be able to improve the economy with a *minimum* of revenue-sharing that is ultimately debilitating to struggling state/provincial and local political units. We must strive always to keep people's money closer to the source from which produces it in the first place. A federal government simply cannot be "all things to all people." It is time that many of the required responsibilities and duties be returned to the state/province along with the necessary tax money to carry these tasks forward to successful conclusion,

a. **I agree** with just about all of the ideas of the ideas expressed in this statement.

b. **I disagree generally** with this statement, To me the tone seems negative. I feel that the federal government should become more involved in the control of business and industry.

c, **I disagree** with the statement. *Laissez faire* capitalism certainly helped this country initially to become strong materially. Now, however, we need somewhat more of a social-welfare state approach to meet the urgent needs of a significant percentage of the people.

d. **I agree generally** with this statement. It seems quite sensible and reasonable. It offers positive recommendations to alleviate some of the ongoing problems that we face.

e. **I disagree strongly**. Much of this statement is reactionary drivel. Some of these ideas may have made some sense back in the 19th century. However, the super-rich and the rich have "gotten away with murder" in North America. We simply have to figure out a way to redistribute the wealth to a reasonable extent. Democratic socialism is the answer.

f. **I agree strongly.** The labor movement and extended welfare programs have had a lot to do with the sad fiscal plight of both the United States and Canada. Budgets should be balanced, but they never will be with so many inadequate, lazy people living off the fat of the land on, for example, huge governmental payrolls. People simply must prepare themselves *and be willing* to work. Maybe being hungry will make them look a little harder for any gainful employment.

Question #9: LAW AND ORDER.
Law and order is:

a. **Necessary to maintain an organized healthy society**. The lack of respect for authority has led to many unfortunate incidents at all levels of society. The Supreme Court in the United States, for example, went too far in interpreting the constitutional rights of criminals. Canada has done the same. Maybe now we'll gradually firm up our defenses against the rising tide of people who have no fear of inadequate punishments that will be meted out to   them.

b. **The emotional slogan of many of those individuals and groups who oppose progressive social change**. Law and order without justice is characteristic of totalitarian societies. There should be no wire tapping at all, for example. Although rioting can't be condoned, it is essential that we attack the causes of such insurrection--not the symptoms of unrest that might be inherent in present society.

c. **Essential if the free countries of the world are to survive this very difficult period**. For a variety of reasons, legislatures and "supreme courts" have gone too far in coddling the truly dangerous criminal offenders without regard to public safety. In some instances, jurisdictions have even gone so far as to pay criminals to reveal where they have hidden bodies of their victims.

d. **The hypocritical slogan of a frightened and decadent society**. The poor and minority groups occasionally strike back at the absolute, but often concealed, viciousness of an exploitive social order. "Law-'n order" tends to mean "keep
Black, multi-ethnic minorities, youth, and immigrants in their place!" We must treat all alike in our society.

e. **The backbone of a free society**. Absolutely no gains should be allowed as a result of rioting and looting with protests that get out of hand. Civil disturbances must be suppressed ruthlessly. Too many "handcuffs" have been placed on members of law-enforcement agencies doing their jobs. Maybe once again women will all be able to walk the streets without fear of molestation.

f. **Necessary in a democratic society, but the words as used by many take on an unpleasant overtone**. Crimes rates of several types are really serious, but we must move positively rather than negatively to reach their causes and then correct them. Prison rehabilitation programs must be improved significantly. I believe that crime rates would go down markedly if competency-based education and more jobs were made available.

Question #10 POPULATION CONTROL.
Please read the following paragraph. Then indicate the strength or your agreement or disagreement with the import of the statement.

The population control is starkly grim today. The situation has become now become so tragic because there are more than six billion people on earth--and the projection figure is nine billion before a declining trend is expected. We are told that all-out cooperative efforts by the major powers in the world simply cannot ward off the massive starvation of peoples that is coming in the years ahead.

Even if nutrition of an adequate nature were somehow to be provided, over-population is also causing staggering problems with water and stream pollution, air pollution, overcrowding in cities, etc. These difficulties will steadily great worse. A crisis of this magnitude must obviously be attacked on all fronts by people of good will worldwide.

The right to abortion should be legalized universally and readily available when there is no desire to carry a fetus through to birth. The sole choice in this matter should rest with the prospective parents (the mother in the final analysis) with advice from a physician when requested.

Coeducational sex education should be carried out in the public schools at the earliest appropriate age. Contraceptive advice , devices when requested, should be readily available and kept at an inexpensive level with governmental subsidy if required. Subsequently, in overpopulated countries, it will probably be necessary to offer positive incentives--or even penalties!--so that the size of families will be curtailed.

Finally, we can't make the point too strongly that this vital matter has a direct relationship to world peace. There is absolutely no time to waste in the implementation of the necessary procedures to carry out the underlying philosophy expressed in the above statements.

a. **Agreement**--The underlying rationality of this statement and the specific steps to be taken represent my position. Action is needed as soon as possible.

b. **Disagreement**--This is a highly personal matter. The government should refrain from direct involvement. The problem may be serious in a relatively small number of countries, but they should be able to solve it with intelligent planning.

c. **Strong Agreement**--This position and the implementation of the accompanying recommendations represent just a beginning. All sorts of additional measures will be needed in the future. For example, why shouldn't we have licensing so that only genetically qualified people will be allowed to bring children into the world?

d. **Strong Disagreement**--this statement is ridiculous! It goes on at length about something that really isn't a problem. If God had meant for people to be controlled as to the number of offspring they may produce, it would have been so. Government has absolutely no right to become involved in such an aspect of a woman's life (or that of her mate). This whole trend should be resisted very strongly.

e. **Agree Generally**--population control is certainly one of the world's problems. We should work to improve the situation at home and encourage other nations to do the same.

f. **Disagree Generally**--Many have expressed concern about this problem, but it really is not as serious as they have indicated. Birth control information should be available on a voluntary basis to those whose religious faith permits such a practice.

Question #11 TRADE UNIONS.

Identify the extent of your agreement or disagreement with the following statement:

The origin, growth, and development of trade unions in North America have been most significant. When the capitalistic system reached a stage where large individual fortunes were being made, certain segments of the working population were finding it next to impossible to realize the material benefits necessary to maintain a reasonable and secure standard of living.

The advances made by unions did not come easily. In fact, the struggle was exceedingly difficult. Often long, bitter strikes were needed before reasonable--not always equitable--settlements were effected. These periodic strikes brought great hardships to many families. The concept of a "closed shop" was a bitter pill for many companies and industries to swallow. It still is for many today. The establishment of a relationship between salary raises and the cost-of-living index did not come easily either. Most helpful to the development of unions was their informal yet strong tie-ins with political parties.

The union movement has spread in many directions. This development has been very helpful to such groups as government workers, teachers, and many other occupations. Union leaders and rank-and-file members should now make strong efforts to recruit members of minority groups, women, and any other needy people at all levels of the business and commercial enterprise. This must be done, even if it becomes necessary to change existing standards temporarily—or perhaps brought about by setting up a larger number of categories. If a capitalistic economy is to exist worldwide, unions must loom large in the struggle for equality of opportunity here and everywhere else.

Unions should continue with the vigorous prosecution of their demands for such benefits as the guaranteed annual wage and other rewards to enable workers to steadily improve their quality of life. The government should not invoke the idea of compulsory arbitration except in most extreme situations to settle longstanding disputes, nor should it subject unions to back-to-work legislation except when a national emergency exists.

a. **Agreement**--This is my position. The union movement gives me hope that the world is a fair place in which to live. Unions have given workers a sense of security and morale that permits them to work more productively and comfortably at the same time.

b. **General Disagreement**--There are some good points here, but this statement gives unions far too much credit and power.

c. **Strong Disagreement**--This is ridiculous. The power of the unions must be curbed before the overall economy is destroyed.

d. **General Agreement**--The unions have helped North American companies, but some of these statements go too far. No group should be allowed to become too powerful.

e. **Disagreement**--This is definitely not my belief about the background and present position of trade unions. Union development needs to be watched carefully for excesses that are apt to creep in.

f. **Strong Agreement**--This statement is good, but the report of accomplishments should be even more glowing. The United States and Canada would not be where they are today if it were not for the magnificent saga of North America's trade unions.

Question #12 HIGHLY COMPETITIVE SPORT.

Please record the extent to which you agree or disagree with the following statement:

Competitive sport was created by people thousands of years ago (presumably) to serve humankind beneficially. It can and does serve a multitude of purposes in today's world. With sound leadership it can good for both boys and girls in their formative years. It can help to develop desirable character and personality traits and also promote vigorous health. It can also provide good role models for young people to emulate. Our states and provinces should get fully behind these activities by providing appropriate competition for young people as they are developing. Such sporting competition should be regarded as supplemental to regular physical activity education programs at all levels of education.

To compete in highly competitive sport today, and do well, it requires extensive, dedicated practice over a period of many years. It is argued that it is important for our countries to be well represented in international competitions and at the Olympic Games. Thus, we should continue to find ways that we can more fully subsidize our young people so that they may strive for, and perhaps ultimately achieve their highest aspirations in this regard. Eventually a small percentage of these athletes will, in addition to the *intrinsic* rewards that sport participation provides, will search for ways to capitalize *extrinsically*, also on any such talent developed. In certain sports particularly enjoyed by society, these young people may even turn professional as such status becomes available to them.

Such a development takes place in a number of other life activities (e.g., music, drama), but in sport in the past, this was somehow contrary to the amateur ideal and the spirit of Olympism. However, holding true to the original Olympic ideal has just about become impossibility today. When the United States, for example, lost the Olympic title in basketball, there evidently could be only one response--bring in the "pros" with their multi-million salaries to trounce those "upstarts." Now even they are having trouble "bringing home the bacon!"

As the Olympic Movement becomes increasingly professionalized at all levels, along with the problem of controlling drug usage to enhance performance, one wonders to what extent present-day practices can be compared to the problems that arose with the ancient Olympic Games.

They were abolished in 776 B.C. because of the excesses that developed. We must search harder for ways to hold this cheating and phony "professionalism" in check? The question arises: Will the modern Games suffer the same fate as those in ancient times for similar reasons?

a.   **Agreement--**This is a very good statement. Sport can indeed be a force for *good* in the world, but we must be very careful to ensure that the *evil present* in many of the prevailing practices that have developed with highly commercialized sport doesn't outweigh any good that might be achieved. We are dangerously close to this now wherever the emphasis is on money largely and not on what is happening to the young man or woman involved. Many of these influences have "trickled down" to certain universities and some schools at the lower levels. We need fine programs of intramural sports for young people in all school.

b.   **Disagreement--**This statement has some merit, but I do not buy this "good and evil" bit as described immediately above. Competitive sport has proved itself an important social influence in society. It is important to have as many "winners" as possible in today's world. It is a "hard" world out there, and people need to know how to compete. In addition, it is vital for our country to do well in international competition including the involvement with the Olympic Games. Further, young people who can earn athletic scholarships for their university education deserve this chance. Additionally, highly competitive sport provides a great deal of entertainment and enjoyment to millions of people as well.

Question #13--GAY AND LESBIAN RELATIONSHIPS. Please read the following statement carefully, and then decide which position or stance is closest to your present values and beliefs.

Morality and ethics have been hot topics from the 1990s on into the new century. *The New York Times* reported, for example, "our morality is disintegrating because its foundation is eroding." The Washington Post asserted, "The core of U.S. national character has been damaged because we've lost our sense of virtue!" Although denying a person's right to choose abortion is still being argued by a minority, the question of gays in the military has been only temporarily (quite unsatisfactorily) resolved in the U.S.A. In addition, we are still finding difficulty in granting full rights as citizens to same-sex alliances. Of course, it does seem reasonable that, if a person is willing to die for his or her country in military service, how this person fulfills sexual desires in the privacy of a bedroom should hardly be a major issue today. Nevertheless, the questions of immorality and its relationship to the legal system are still present and will not go away easily.

John Kekes, a U.S. philosopher, calls the argument that "the world is going to Hell in a hand basket," morally speaking, The *Disintegration Thesis*. The position is as follows:

(1) The value system of the culture no longer offers significant rationale for subordinating one's self to the common good.
(2) A healthy democratic government depends on values that come from religion (the Judeo-Christian tradition that is).
(3) Human rights are based on the moral worth that a loving God has granted to each human soul.
(4) Authority in social affairs is empowered because of underlying transcendent moral law (Brookings Institution).

What this all adds up to is that the Disintegration Thesis holds since society's basic problem is moral. What rebuttal may be offered to the idea that our culture is sliding down a slippery slope to moral bankruptcy? Kekes argues that the whole problem is simply this: Moral change has been confused with moral disintegration. He agrees that are many seemingly disturbing moral issues today, but he then inquires about the significance of these facts as a "new morality" struggles to be born. What is being abandoned is the idea that there is one and only one set of virtues for a human life--One *Summum Bonum,* to place the dilemma in terms of Latin.

However, the Disintegration Thesis argument is that a gradual change in our morality has been occurring, and that such change will continue into the future. However, in this change from a single morality to a pluralistic one in North America, there are still many good traits or virtues present in our daily lives. We still have the basic concepts of freedom, knowledge, happiness, justice, love, order, privacy, wisdom, etc. with which to guide and develop our personal lives and social living. However, we should understand that in this ever-increasing pluralistic culture none of these concepts is necessarily reducible to the other--and especially not to the idea that there is one transcendental moral law. This means that each person should work in his or her life for some reasonable or acceptable combination of such values as love, freedom, justice, etc.

a. **Agreement**. I find myself essentially in agreement with the position taken immediately above by the writer. Times are indeed changing, and we simply must be fair to *all* concerned. A number of the concerns expressed about gay and lesbian relationships are not central to "the good life"--they are peripheral. What is important in life is that we should be fair, decent, and just in our relationships with others--not that we should concern ourselves with people's sexual preferences. A spectrum seems to exist about the "maleness" or "femaleness" of a person, a condition that is inherent in that individual and cannot be altered without maladjustment occurring.

b. **Disagreement.** This "NEW" morality sounds great and may be fine to those individuals ready to accept the changes that are occurring toward a pluralistic morality. However, as a defender of The Disintegration Thesis, this argument for acceptance of such an oddly emerging situation simply adds fuel to the fire. Any individually selected amalgam of values and virtues represents just one more symptom of the moral bankruptcy that is taking place right before our eyes. The advocates of a new, more pluralistic morality, if they hope to win their argument, must show that there is sufficient continuity between the old and the new, between monistic and pluralistic morality.

Question #14 ENVIRONMENTAL CRISIS.

Please read the following statement. Then decide which of the two statements below is closest to your stance or belief about the problem outlined.

Ecology is defined as the field of study that treats the relationships and interactions of human beings and other living organisms with each other and with their natural environment. Since 1975, interest in this vital subject has increased steadily and markedly with each passing year. Nevertheless, the "say-do" gap in relation to truly doing something about Earth's plight in this regard is enormous.

What, then, is the extent of the environmental crisis in modern society? Very simply, we have achieved a certain mastery over the world because of our scientific and technological achievement. We are at the top of the food chain because of our mastery of much of Earth's flora and fauna. However, because of the explosion of the human population, increasingly greater pressures "will be placed on our lands to provide shelter, food, recreation, and waste disposal areas. This will cause a greater pollution of the atmosphere, the rivers, the lakes, the land, and the oceans" (Mergen). This bleak picture could be expanded; yet, perhaps the tide will soon turn. Certainly many recognize the gravity of prevailing patterns of human conduct, but a great many more people must develop attitudes that will lead them to take positive action in the immediate future. It is time for concerted global action, and we can only hope that it is not too late to reverse the effects of a most grave situation.

We can all appreciate the difficulty of moving from a scientific "is" to an ethical "ought" in the realm of human affairs. There are obviously many scientific findings within the environmental sciences that should be made available to people of all ages. Simply making the facts available, of course, will not be any guarantee that strong and positive attitudes will develop on the subject. It is a well-established fact, however, that the passing of legislation in difficult and sensitive areas must take place through responsible political leadership, and that attitude changes often follow behind, albeit at what may seem to be a snail's pace.

The field of education should play a vital role now, as it has never done before, in the development of what might be called an "ecological awareness." Obviously, this has become much broader than it was earlier because the field of ecology now places all of the individual entities of Earth in a total context in which the interrelationship of all parts must be thoroughly understood. If the field of education has a strong obligation to present the various issues revolving about the newly understood need for the development of an ecological awareness, this duty obviously includes all who are employed within the educational system, have a certain general education responsibility to all participants in their classes or programs.

Presumably, this matter cannot be called a persistent problem historically. The overwhelming magnitude of poor ecological practices has not been even partially understood by the general populace. Now some realize the urgency of the matter, but others are telling them that further study is needed, that the ecologists are exaggerating, and that they are simply pessimistic by nature.

a. **Agreement.** I find myself in essential agreement with the underlying position taken by the writer above. This is a crisis because the need for "ecological awareness" is racing headlong into a collision with growing worldwide capitalism in the burgeoning global economy. The time is now to take drastic steps to alleviate and/or resolve this overwhelmingly difficult problem.

b. **Disagreement**. The writer makes some good points, of course. We must be ever vigilant as to elements and forces (also companies and people) that are careless and/or dishonest in their "relations" with the environment. However, if a country seeks to do conscientiously what it can to alleviate problems that develop, that should do the trick. The earth is resilient. This is one of a number of important and issues the world is facing.

Question #15 CLONING AND CELLULAR RESEARCH. Please read the statement below. Then record your agreement or disagreement as you did with previous questions.

In the 21st century, using a Biblical-quoting rationale based on Genesis (IV), to castigate scientists for "staggering arrogance" in presuming to play God by conducting cloning research does not cut much ice. (Note that god is spelled with a capital "G.") As the argument proceeds, none other than the eminent philosopher/theologian, George W. Bush, bolsters the strength of this argument. Does the author actually think that this former Yale "scholar" personally wrote--and indeed meant! --the words he spoke? "As we seek what is possible, we must also ask what is right--and we must not forget that even the most noble ends do not justify any means".

In response, here is a thought for our nay saying friends to absorb early in this new millennium. Your Christian God has a tough struggle ahead to keep its status as the number #1 life force in a multiethnic world. The world society is just too replete with its many versions of "The Great One." This is becoming ever more true as both Europeans and North Americans struggle with their own rapidly increasing, multiethnic cultural incursions. Each has its "unique" version of the Almighty.

When it comes to this question of cellular and cloning research, the voices of the clerics involved come through as a "vast pooling of ignorance." They speak as though they *know* what is right and what is wrong. They know, you see, because God told them so! The fact of the matter is that neither they--nor do any of the rest of us as their often gullible listeners-- really know what is right and what is wrong anymore. Their hoary dogma simply does not "do it" today.

Unless knowledge of "how it all began" somehow becomes known to humankind–and can we really believe this will ever happen? --we earthlings do not have much choice. We must figure out--working together! --what's "right" action and what's "wrong" action for us in the 21st century. Our decisions quite simply must be *based on our own life experience*. If we do not manage to do this, ultimate disaster to life as we know it today seems almost inevitable. The handwriting is on the wall!

Cross-cultural understanding must be cultivated with great diligence. This is vital because our "global village" with its blanketing communications network is steadily bringing about similar values and norms of conduct worldwide. The world needs to view solutions to ethical dilemmas such as cloning and cellular research in a similar manner. Such an approach to ethical decision-making could well be the only hope for human life to continue successfully on Earth in the future.

a. **Agreement**.   Findings from the scientific community keep flooding in. Some are good, some debatable, and some turn out to be wrong. Life moves on in often strange and mysterious ways. It appears to be an open-ended universe. We do not really know where we came from, or where we are going. Scientific discoveries and the medical profession backed by the health sciences have lengthened the average length of human life. Now we are promised even better length and longevity through cellular research. I say, "Go for it!"

b. **Disagreement**.   How far should humans go in tampering with life processes? When a man and woman are married and subsequently procreate, they are in tune with the plan that the Creator has preordained for humans and all other living creatures on earth. Humans should not tamper with His plan for us. Abortion, for example, is a sin against humankind. Using cloned creatures for "spare parts" when or where needed is not my idea of how humans should behave.

Question #16. UNIVERSAL HEALTH CARE

Please read the statement below. Then record your agreement or disagreement as you did with previous questions.

So-called "universal health care" is now a great problem for countries of the world to solve. This is so because the expense of paying for all sorts of medical expenses, including some based on incomplete scientific backing, has become prohibitive. To pay for everything "eats up" a "disproportionate" amount of as country's overall budget.

In North America, for example, the United States has a situation in which some 45% of the population has no medical coverage. In addition, it is not known what percentage of the remainder have policies that provide that could be termed "inadequate" coverage. Often when a specific claim is made, the response is that either coverage is not available on the existing policy, or that only a percentage of the needed amount will be paid.

The Canadian situation is different in that all bona fide residents have universal health care. However, provision of such "universality" is now a problem of increasing concern because of the enormous expense involved. Fortunately, all life-threatening illnesses are cared for as "emergencies" at the first possible moment. However, it is "elective" surgery and other "non-emergency" care that have become a problem because of long waiting periods for treatment. In addition, each province has different arrangements as to which "unproven," but possibly helpful service or medication will be covered under the medical insurance plan.

A further issue has arisen as well. Private agencies are developing plans whereby people with the necessary means can get treatment for so-called "elective" medical problems much sooner that if they simply waited their turn. A variation of this view of the issue is a scheme whereby a person can get insurance to cover his/her expense (and that of a companion) to travel to the United States for treatment IF service is not available in Canada after a specified period.

Everything considered, in the 21st country a North American country ought to provide full medical coverage for all of its citizens regardless of their ability to pay. Not to do so creates a situation in which the needs of rich people are met in one way or another, The needs of the middle-class may be met, but some times by incurring long term-debt. In addition, the poor simply "fade away" and die sooner. The only fair and just conclusion is that the total expense should be borne by the government through its taxation scheme.

a. **Agreement.** I believe that medical coverage should be "complete" for *all* to the greatest possible extent. The time has past when a modern country should have "first-class" citizens and "second-class" citizens when it comes to a person's health and wellbeing.

b. **Disagreement**. I certainly do not want to see people suffer unnecessarily or die because of inadequate medical care. However, government simply cannot be "all things to all people at all times." People have to learn to become responsible citizens. They need to plan their budgets carefully so that they and their families will be provided for in the various circumstances that arise. Emergency coverage is one thing that the government should be responsible for, but complete insurance coverage for all sorts of elective medical services is more than a person has a right to expect in our society.

Question #17. EDUCATIONAL AIMS & OBJECTIVES
The fundamental aim of education is:

a. Education should seek to "awaken awareness" in the learner (i.e., awareness of the person as a single subjectivity in the world. Increased emphasis is needed on the arts and social sciences, and the student should freely and creatively choose his or her own pattern of education. Socialization of the child has become equally as important as his or her intellectual development as a key educational aim in this century.

b. Social-self-realization is the supreme value in education. The realization of this ideal is most important for the individual in the social setting--a world culture. Positive ideals should be molded toward the evolving democratic ideal by a general education that is group-centered and in which the majority determines the acceptable goals. However, once that majority opinion is determined, all are obligated to conform until such majority opinion can be reversed (the doctrine of "defensible partiality").

c. The concept of 'education' has become much more complex that was ever realized before. Because of the various meanings of the term "education," talking about educational aims and objectives is almost a hopeless task unless a myriad of qualifications is used for clarification. We need to qualify our meaning to explain to the listener whether we mean (1) the subject-matter; (2) the activity of education carried on by teachers; (3) the process of being educated (or learning) that is occurring; (4) the result, actual or intended, or No.2 and No.3 Immediately above taking place through the employment of that which comprises No.1 above; (5) the discipline, or field of enquiry and investigation; and (6) the profession whose members are involved professionally with all of the aspects of education described above. With this understanding, it is then possible to make some determination about which specific objectives the profession of education should strive for as it moves in the direction of the achievement of long range aims.

d. The general aim of education is more education. Education in the broadest sense can be nothing else than the changes made in human beings by their experience. Participation by students in the formation of aims and objectives is essential to generate the all-important desired interest required for the finest educational process to occur. Social efficiency (i.e., societal socialization) should be considered the general aim of education. Pupil growth is a paramount goal. This means that the individual is placed at the center of the educational experience.

e. The aim of education is the acquisition of verified knowledge of the individual's environment. This aim recognizes the value of content as well as the activities involved; and also takes into account the external determinants of human behavior. Education is the acquisition of the art of the utilization of knowledge. The primary task of education is to transmit knowledge, knowledge without which civilization could not continue to flourish. Some holding this philosophy believe that the good life emanates from cooperation with God's grace, and believe further that the development of these virtues is obviously of greater worth than learning or anything else.

f. Through education the developing organism becomes what it latently is. All education has a religious significance, the meaning of which is that there is a "moral imperative" on education. As the person's mind strives to realize itself, there is the possibility of the Absolute within the individual mind. Education should aid the child to adjust to the basic realities (the spiritual ideals of truth, beauty, and goodness) that the history of the race has furnished us. The basic values of human living are health, character, social justice, skill, art, love, knowledge, philosophy, and religion.

++

See next page for scoring instructions

Check your answers with the following Score Sheet. With each question write in the appropriate number of points scored (*as plus or minus*) where indicated.

Question

1. a. +3
    b. +2
    c. +1
    d. -1 _____
    e. -2 score
    f. -3

2. a. +3
    b. +1
    c. -2
    d. +2 _____
    e. -1 score
    f. -3

3. a. -3
    b. -2
    c. -1
    d. +1 _____
    e. +2 score
    f. +3

4. a. -3
    b. +3
    c. -2
    d. +1 _____
    e. +2 score
    f. -1

5. a. +3
    b. -2
    c. +1 _____
    d. -3 score
    e. +2
    f. -1

Question

6. a. -2
    b. +2
    c. -1
    d. +1 _____
    e. +3 score
    f. -3

7. a. +2
    b. -1
    c. -2
    d. +1 _____
    e. -3 score
    f. +3

8. a. +2
    b. -1
    c. -2
    d. +1 _____
    e. -3 score
    f. +3

9. a. +1
    b. -1
    c. +2
    d. -3 _____
    e. +3 score
    f. -2

10. a. -2
    b. +2
    c. -3
    d. -1 _____
    e. +1 score
    f. +3

11.   a.   -2
         b.   +1
         c.   +3
         d.   -1   _____
         e.   +2   score
         f.   -3

14.   a.   -3
         b.   +3   _____
                      score

12.   a.   +3
         b.   -3
         c.   -2
         d.   +1   _____
         e.   -1   score
         f.   +2

15.   a.   -3
         b.   +3   _____
                      score

13.   a.   -3
         b.   +3   _____
                      score

16.   a.   -3
         b.   +3   _____
                      score

17.   a.   -1 (Existentialistic)
         b.   -2 (Somewhat Progressive)
         c.   -0 (Analytic)
         d.   -3 (Progressive)
         e.   +3 (Traditional   _____
               (including Strongly Traditional Elements) score
         f.   +2 (Traditional)

B. Add your plus (+) scores together (if any)……...Total = _____

C. Add your minus (-) scores together (if any)…….Total = _____

D. Subtract the smaller score (plus or minus) from the larger one.

It may be, of course, that you will have just one cumulative plus or minus score. In this case, no subtraction is necessary.

Your resultant total could conceivable be zero (0).
It is more likely, however, that it will either be plus "something" (e.g., plus [+] 9) or minus "something" (e.g., minus (-) 14.

E. The result is your **S**ocio-**P**olitical **Q**uotient (either conservative **+ SPQ** or liberal **- SPQ**.

Note: Of course, *this is not a good nor alternatively, a bad score--whatever it is!*

Discussion

Your score could range from plus 51 to minus 51. There is a world of difference between these two extremes. The scale below is a rough approximation indicating the range of socio-political "positions." Six such positions have been identified for the purposes of this self-evaluation questionnaire.

It has been argued that a country needs both socio-political conservatives **and** liberals. Progressives are anxious to see implemented what they regard as beneficial, while conservatives want to make certain that such change being recommended is desirable and possibly beneficial **before** they accept it.

A score somewhere around the zero (0) mark is difficult to assess. It probably indicates someone who is a middle-of-the-road person, perhaps a fence sitter on controversial issues. However, it might indicate someone who has varying positions on both sides of the spectrum--and whose scores simply balance each other out. This would be the position of an eclectic, but not what has been termed a patterned eclectic.

+36 to +51 = (Reactionary)

+22 to +35 = (Conservative)

+7 to +21 = (Moderate Conservative)

+6 to -6   =   (Middle of the Road: Eclectic or *Maverick?***])**

-7 to -21   =   (Moderate Liberal

-22 to -35 =   (Liberal)

-36 to -51   =   (Radical)

Appendix C
How Do You Rate Yourself Recreationally?
(An "RQ" Test for Self-Evaluation)

Throughout history all societies have misused leisure after they struggled long and hard to earn it. In certain instances the misuse of free time has actually caused the downfall of that society.

North Americans have been accused of having spectatoritis (that is, spending too much of their free time watching others taking part in some form of recreation).

Many people are concerned about whether they are getting sufficient pleasure out of life. Here is an opportunity to determine your overall "recreational quotient" based on involvement (or lack of same) in a variety of recreational pursuits.

This simple, self-evaluative test for adults of all ages was developed so that men and women could rate themselves recreationally and then take steps as they wish to improve their "recreational quotient." There is no doubt but that sound recreational pursuits can add zest and vigor to our lives.

We can all appreciate that there are many ways of looking at the subject of recreation. However, although we could determine averages (or norms) for a given population in regard to types of recreational pursuits followed, it doesn't seem advisable to try to set standards in a free society.

Of course, one development of modern society has been that people are increasingly crowded together in heavily populated urban and suburban communities. This creates a problem: How can people find happiness, satisfaction, and a high quality of life despite and increased tempo of living and increasing crowded conditions?

In taking this test, or carrying out this self-evaluation, please answer the questions as honestly and frankly as possible. The test is based on a scale moving from passive, to vicarious, to active, to creative involvement in life's many educational/recreational activities. It gives you more credit if you are a <u>most interested</u> onlooker or listener rather than a <u>passive</u> one. Moreover, you will score even higher if you <u>actively</u> take part in a particular recreational activity. The highest rating goes to the person who participates in a superior and/or creative fashion.

INSTRUCTIONS:

Give yourself one point if you answer "yes" to question No.1 under sports and physical recreational interests. In like manner give yourself two points for answering question No.2 affirmatively, three points for question No.3, and four points for No.4. The maximum score for each category is ten points.

At the bottom of each section (or category of recreational interest), total your score from each of the four questions in that section. When you have completed all of the questions in the five categories, total the scores from the different categories.

Finally, rate yourself according to the scale for your grand total, and also according to the scale for individual sections. Although in developing this self-evaluation scale, we did give you more points for active involvement, we are not seeking to establish an overall standard for participation.

After you have completed this assessment and determined your recreational quotient ("RQ"), we will offer some suggestions and recommendations for your consideration.

CATEGORY I: Sports and Physical Activity (e.g., golf, bowling, aerobics class)

1. Do you regularly at least glance through the sports section of your local newspaper?

    Yes ( ) or No ( )..................... Score _____

2. Are you a faithful follower of at least one team or athlete, rejoicing in victory and fretting in defeat?

    Yes ( ) or No ( )..................... Score _____

3. Do you take part at least two or three times a week through-out the entire in regular physical activity (e.g., an active

game or sport, brisk walking for a mile)

Yes ( ) or No ( )..................... Score _____

4. Are you considered one of the better players in any active
    physical activity or active game or sport among opponents
    your own age?

Yes ( ) or No ( )..................... Score _____

Total Score for this Section............... Score _____

Scale

10 pts. --- superior
6 pts. --- good
3 pts. --- fair
1 pt. --- poor

CATEGORY II: Social Activities (e.g., social club,
            church program, family recreation)

1. Do you take pleasure in make nodding acquaintances and exchanging
    the time of day with a number of people?

Yes ( ) or No ( )..................... Score _____

2. Do you take an interest in and attend at least one social club
    or organization regularly?

Yes ( ) or No ( )..................... Score _____

3. Do you invite friends in for dinner or a social get-together
    (or invite someone out) at least once a month?

Yes ( ) or No ( )..................... Score _____

4. In the past year have you been elected an officer or served
    as a committee chairperson of a club or a social or political
    organization?

Yes ( ) or No ( )..................... Score _____

Total Score for this Section................ Score _____
(See scale under Sport & Physical Activity)

CATEGORY III: Communicative Activities (e.g., article writing, letter to editor, speaking, discussion group)

1. Do you telephone or drop in on a friend regularly just to pass the time of day?

Yes ( ) or No ( )..................... Score _____

2. Do you argue for a point of view even though it may mean a difference of opinion with a close friend or committee chairperson?

Yes ( ) or No ( )..................... Score _____

3. Have you in the past six months written one or more letters strongly expressing your opinion to an editor, school principal, or civic official?

Yes ( ) or No ( )..................... Score _____

4. In the past year have you given a talk or led discussion at your PTA, church, or any other local group?

Yes ( ) or No ( )..................... Score _____

Total Score for this Section................ Score _____

CATEGORY IV: Aesthetic & Creative Activities ("Cultural") (e.g., oil painting, music, sculpting)

1. Do you like to listen to a musical concert or watch a serious drama on television?

Yes ( ) or No ( )..................... Score _____

2. Have you attended at least three or four concerts, play, or art exhibits in the past year?

Yes ( ) or No ( )...................... Score _____

3. Do you paint, sketch, play an instrument, or sing, etc. regularly?

Yes ( ) or No ( )...................... Score _____

4. If your answer to #3 immediately above, do you rate yourself sufficiently high to enter a content or competition?

Yes ( ) or No ( )...................... Score _____

Total Score for this Section............... Score _____

CATEGORY V: Educational Activities (e.g., hobbies such as ham radio, gardening, astronomy, coin-collecting)

1. Do you like to hear or read about the learning interests of others?

Yes ( ) or No ( ).................... Score _____

2. Are you so interested and knowledgeable in any educational or recreational hobby (apart from one you are engaged in yourself) that you could discuss it intelligently with an expert on the subject?

Yes ( ) or No ( ).................... Score _____

3. Do you have a "learning-interest" hobby of your own in which you are involved regularly?

Yes ( ) or No ( ).................... Score _____

4. Are you considered an expert on your hobby, one to whom others may turn for advice, and possibly having won an award or special

mention in the past year or two?

Yes ( ) or No ( )..................... Score _____

<u>Total Score</u> for this Section............... Score _____

NOW ADD UP THE TOTAL FOR EACH CATEGORY TO GET YOUR GRAND TOTAL--<u>YOUR FINAL SCORE</u> = _____

<u>ANALYSIS</u>: Now rate yourself according to the following scale:

50-35 pts.--<u>Outstanding</u>--You may be getting too much fun and pleasure out of life. How about doing some more constructive work for a change?
34-24 pts.--<u>Above Average</u>--You may have achieved a balance between work and play in your life. You are evidently enjoying your leisure without having a guilty conscience.
23-14 pts.--<u>Average</u>--Your score indicate a fair status. You may be somewhat narrow or one-sided, or you may not have achieved much depth in anything. Check this out keeping the ideal in mind.
13-6 pts.--<u>Below Average</u>--You are missing some of the good things, the pleasurable activities, that life has to offer. Review and assess your goals for living.
5-0 pts.--<u>Poor</u>--Life is undoubtedly a tedious routine for you. <u>Wake up and live</u>!

<u>RECOMMENDATIONS / SUGGESTIONS</u>:

This assessment of your personal "recreational quotient," obviously a subjective evaluation, is based on the premise that you should determine intelligently and carefully what it is that you want out of life. What do you value in your life?

Some might say they want pleasure, knowledge, and prestige, while others might stress creativity, adventure, and good health. A third group might wish for improvement of certain personality traits, a renewal of religious faith, and a continued capacity to profit from a lifelong education.

However you may rank your personal values in descending order, there is solid evidence that choosing a sound educational/recreational pattern in your life is difficult and should be an ever-changing challenge throughout life.

The premise upon which this entire self-evaluation is based in that the specific decisions you make about which free-time activities you will be involved with--and how you go about carrying them out--can mean a great deal toward the achievement of your life goals.

Some people are lucky enough to have a career in which they can find the satisfactions which coincide with many of their chosen values. But you may not a position where this is possible. This is why it is so important for you to establish your own hierarchy of values and then to select your educational/recreational pattern of living. We wish you well in this quest. . .
.